The
SPIRIT AND POWER
of
Elijah

MICHELLE McCLAIN-WALTERS

CHARISMA
HOUSE

THE SPIRIT AND POWER OF ELIJAH by Michelle
McClain-Walters
Published by Charisma House, an imprint of Charisma Media
600 Rinehart Road, Lake Mary, Florida 32746

While the author has made every effort to provide accurate,
up-to-date source information at the time of publication,
statistics and other data are constantly updated. Neither the
publisher nor the author assumes any responsibility for errors or

for changes that occur after publication. Further, the publisher and author do not have any control over and do not assume any responsibility for third-party websites or their content.

For more resources like this, visit charismahouse.com and MichelleMcclainWalters.shop.

Cataloging-in-Publication Data is on file with the Library of Congress.

International Standard Book Number: 978-1-63641-158-3

E-book ISBN: 978-1-63641-160-6

1 2023

Printed in the United States of America

Most Charisma Media products are available at special quantity discounts for bulk purchase for sales promotions, premiums, fund-raising, and educational needs. For details, call us at (407) 333-0600 or visit our website at www.charismamedia.com.

Contents

Introduction

THROUGHOUT HUMAN HISTORY, there arise certain figures whose stories resonate across time and culture, illuminating a path of faith and righteousness with a radiant glow. Among these towering figures, the biblical prophet Elijah stands as a beacon, his narrative an exquisite tapestry woven with divine encounters, unwavering conviction, and miraculous interventions. Yet Elijah is not merely a relic of the past; he is a living testament to the enduring relationship between humanity and the Spirit of God.

Within the pages of this book, we embark on a transformative journey through the life, ministry, and legacy of this remarkable prophet. We will look deep into his character and discover the passions that set his heart ablaze, the faith that propelled him into action, and the profound encounters with God that defined his destiny.

Elijah's story transcends mere historical documentation; it is a revelation of the limitless potential that emerges when the human spirit converges with the power of God. It is a testament to the relentless fire of faith that can ignite even in the darkest of circumstances, dispelling the shadows of doubt and fear.

But this book is far more than an exploration of the past; it is a divine summons to embrace the spirit and power of Elijah within our own lives. It is a declaration that the same God who answered with fire on Mount Carmel is still listening to the fervent prayers of His people today. It beckons us to awaken the Elijah within us, to seek divine encounters, and to boldly confront the idols and injustices of our era.

As we examine the mosaic of Elijah's life, we are reminded that the spirit and power of this prophet are within reach for all who dare to believe. The God who endowed Elijah with the authority to command the elements, defy the status quo, and stand unwavering in his faith is the very same God inviting us into His presence today.

Prepare to be inspired and ignited. Brace yourself to plumb the depths of your own faith and explore the possibilities that unfold when you dare to believe in the God of Elijah. *The Spirit and Power of Elijah* is not just an historical account; it is the unveiling of a living, breathing faith that transcends the confines of time—a faith that compels us to stand boldly in the face of adversity and proclaim as the people in Elijah's day did, "The LORD, He is God!" (1 Kings 18:39).

May this exploration of the spirit and power of Elijah set your spirit ablaze, awaken your unwavering conviction, and embolden you to confront the challenges of your time with resolute determination.

PART 1
REVIVAL

Chapter 1

Repairer of the Breach, Revealer of Hearts

THE FIRE OF revival is coming.

I believe revival is coming now, for this generation. We will not die but live and declare the works of the Lord. We will see the glory of the Lord manifested on the earth. We will see an outpouring of revival that will change hearts, change lives, change families, change communities, change cities, change nations, and change the world. Are you ready?

There was a time in Israel's history characterized by idolatry, declining morality, and a turning away from the one true God. Israel was in need of revival. The people of Israel were in need of a call to repentance. They were in need of reformation. They were in need of restoration. So the Lord sent a prophet named Elijah.

We are now living in a time characterized by idolatry, declining morality, and a turning away from the one true God. We are in need of revival. We are in need of a call to repentance. We are in need of reformation. We are in need of restoration. So the Lord is sending Elijahs. A new company of Elijahs is being raised up. A new company of prophets—holy, bold, and uncompromising—is being equipped to restore the spiritual destiny of the church in this generation. Are you an Elijah?

THE DAYS OF ELIJAH

During the days of the prophet Elijah, the king of Israel was a man named Ahab. The Bible says "there was no one like Ahab who sold himself to do wickedness in the sight of the LORD, because Jezebel his wife stirred him up" (1 Kings 21:25).

Led by Ahab and Jezebel, the people of Israel turned away from the Lord. Instead of worshipping the one true God, they worshipped idols and false gods. The worship of these false gods included sexual perversion, child sacrifice, and other things that grieved the heart of the Lord and opposed His plan for His people. The nation of Israel had fallen away from the Lord in the years since they had been rescued from slavery in Egypt and brought to the Promised Land, and the moral decline intensified during the reign of Ahab and Jezebel.

As it was in the days of Elijah, today a great number of God's people dwell in a nation that is on a path of progressive decline in morality. Certain US states have among the most liberal abortion standards in the world. From 1973 to 2017, almost sixty million babies in the US were aborted.[1] Millions of people, including many in the church, are hooked on pornography.[2] The homosexual agenda and gay marriage are finding acceptance even in the church. Divorce continues to tear apart families, both in the church and out. Human trafficking is front and center, manifesting as the ugly side of globalization. Those considered great leaders are now preaching a doctrine of inclusion. Christian leaders are afraid to say on national television that Jesus Christ is the only way to salvation. We are falling away from the Lord and bearing the fallout of it.

As a new decade began in 2020, the world was plagued with disease, sickness, violence, financial problems, and many other major issues. In the midst of turmoil and crisis, the people of God were crying out, "Why weren't we warned?" They were crying out for the prophets to speak. Ezekiel 7:26 says, "Disaster will come upon disaster, and rumor will be upon rumor. Then they will seek a vision from a prophet." But the truth is that the prophets have already been speaking, just as they had been in Ezekiel's day. And just as happened time and time again when the prophets of Israel spoke, the people did not heed the word of the Lord. But that doesn't mean God has given up on His people.

Sometimes it takes a season of trouble for people to turn to God.

THE SEASON OF TROUBLE

In the season of trouble we have been facing over the last few years, God has heard the cries of His people. In response to the cries of His people and out of His love for them, God is raising up a new company of prophets. He is equipping them with the spiritual fortitude to restore the destiny of the church in this generation. To discover whom God will send in a time like the one we are experiencing now, we must ask ourselves: What prophet from the Bible would God send to us today in the twenty-first century? Who do we need in this hour?

In a time when Israel was caught up in idolatry and desecration of the holy places of God, no prophet could arise and do what needed to be done other than Elijah. God called and then developed Elijah to be the challenging force against the unmatched wickedness of his day.

The anointing that God laid upon Elijah's life was geared specifically toward challenging the loyalty of the human heart. It was uniquely designed to change the culture by changing the values of the people at that time. This is the central element of the spirit and power of Elijah: to turn hearts back to God. In this way, the Elijah anointing comes to confront fatherlessness in this generation, setting the lonely in families and calling the generations back to their true identity and destiny in the kingdom of God. As exemplified in the miracle of raising the widow's son back to life (1 Kings 17:17–24), the Elijah anointing has the power to raise the sons of God back to life in Christ.

The Elijah anointing asks a key question: How long will you falter between two opinions? This anointing offends the mind to reveal the heart (Matt. 11:6). God is calling forth prophets with the heart of Elijah to stand boldly against churches of compromise and temples of tolerance. These men and women will be outspoken, unreserved, frank, and candid. They will come with a clear presentation of the gospel and will not be ambiguous or unintelligible. Their boldness and clarity will not come out of their own strength but instead will be the result of being filled with the unction and zeal of the Holy Spirit.

Just as Elijah came against Ahab, Jezebel, and the prophets of Baal, today's Elijah prophets will challenge and confront all illegal spiritual authority. They will operate in miracles, signs, and wonders, testifying of the power, presence, and vengeance of God against idolatry in all its forms.

The miracles of Elijah will not happen in a vacuum. God acts on the earth in response to prayer. Elijah prophets access the Spirit and power of God through persistent prayer (Jas. 5:16–18) and fasting, making tremendous power available to them so that when they pray, they too will have the ability to open and shut the heavens.

As these prophets build spiritual altars in worship and prayer to God, He will release manifestations of power—great might and force—giving them the right, the authority, to act and govern the heavens.

Elijah's anointing broke through four hundred years of

religion, ritualistic worship and tradition, backsliding, and hard-ness of heart. We need this level of power in operation today. The Elijah generation arising today will set life back on course and speak forth destiny into the lives of individuals, families, cities, nations, and generations. It will restore the broken pathways of righteousness and help prepare the way for God's purposes.

WHO IS ELIJAH?

Names in the Bible are really important. Names carry a lot of meaning, whether it is the name given to a child at birth or a new name given to someone by the Lord, as when Jacob became Israel or Saul became Paul. Names often give us insight into a person's character, purpose, or calling.

When Elijah was born, his parents made a bold declaration of faith in the name they chose for their son. Elijah means "my God is Jehovah" or "Jehovah is God."[3] In a time when Baal worship was so prevalent, Elijah's parents weren't afraid to stand against the status quo. They weren't afraid to be bold believers in a society that had turned away from belief in the Lord. In the face of a culture that had fallen away from the Lord, they were saying they had no tolerance for wickedness and idolatry. Elijah's very name was a rebuke of Baal worshippers.

Elijah's name set him apart. His name was a call to holiness, a call to walk in the will of God, a call to pursue righteousness and seek the face of the Lord even when the culture around him was going crazy. It declared the truth—that the Lord is God—and also declared that Elijah was going to live accord-ing to that truth, because his God was the Lord.

Elijah was a Tishbite. While the meaning of the word *Tishbite* is uncertain, it is thought to be associated with the Hebrew verb *shub*. Shub means to turn around, to return, to turn back, or to restore. While it can refer to a physical return, it is often used in reference to a spiritual return or restoration.[4]

> All the ends of the world shall remember and *turn* to the LORD.
>
> —PSALM 22:27, EMPHASIS ADDED

> *RESTORE* us, O God; cause Your face to shine, and we shall be saved!
>
> —PSALM 80:3, EMPHASIS ADDED

> And the ransomed of the LORD shall *return*, and come to Zion with singing, with everlasting joy on their heads. They shall obtain joy and gladness, and sorrow and sighing shall flee away.
>
> —ISAIAH 35:10, EMPHASIS ADDED

Part of Elijah's role was to call the people to repentance. And to repent means to turn from sin, to turn back from doing evil, and to be restored to a right relationship with the Lord. The Elijah anointing turns hearts back to God.

CHARACTERISTICS OF THE ELIJAH ANOINTING

The primary purpose of the Elijah anointing is to turn hearts back to the Lord. It boldly asks a vital question: How long will you falter between two opinions? Because of the boldness of the Elijah anointing in asking such a critical question, this anointing will cause offense.

Jesus warned us that people would be offended because of Him. John the Baptist sent two of his disciples to ask Jesus if He was really the Messiah, and Jesus said, "Go and tell John the things which you hear and see: The blind see and the lame walk; the lepers are cleansed and the deaf hear; the dead are raised up and the poor have the gospel preached to them. And blessed is he who is not offended because of Me" (Matt. 11:4–6). Even in the face of indisputable miracles, people were offended by Jesus, and it is the same today. In fact, I think we are living in a generation of offense, when so many people are offended by anything and everything. We live in a culture that is so over-the-top worried about offending people that we often don't speak the truth, even in love, but the truth needs to be spoken. Remember that the Lord will offend the mind to reveal the heart. He will offend the flesh to reveal the best of a person's spirit.

So many people want God without Jesus, but it doesn't work that way. God is Jesus, and Jesus is God. They cannot be separated. Jesus said He is *the* way, *the* truth, and *the* life (John 14:6). He didn't say He was *a* way, *a* truth, and *a* life. But this generation wants to come up with their own way, their own truth. How many times have you heard people refer to "my truth"? But that is relative truth, and we don't need relative truth. We need absolute truth. We need *the* truth, and the truth is Jesus. And since Jesus is the living Word of God, we know that the Word of God is the truth too.

The Elijah anointing turns the hearts of God's children back to Him. It causes you to think deeply about and wrestle with the truth. And when you wrestle with the truth, it will reveal what is really in your heart. There is no hiding behind cultural norms or the spirit of offense when you come face-to-face with the truth.

But God isn't revealing the truth of what is in your heart for the purpose of offending you or condemning you or beating you down or making you miserable. He reveals the truth of what is in your heart because He loves you and wants what is best for you. And living according to what the world says is true and right is not what is best for you. Remember that the enemy's plan is to have you live a life of deception that will lead you to hell. The spirit and power of Elijah confronts false doctrines and concepts.

Those with the Elijah anointing will confront wickedness and challenge motives of the heart. They need to speak the truth with clarity, boldness, and courage, but they also need to speak the truth in love. The Word says it is the kindness of the Lord that leads us to repentance. You are called to speak the truth, but you are called to speak it with a spirit of love and grace, not a spirit of judgment or condemnation. The Elijah anointing will confront wickedness and idolatry because of the fear of the Lord. Elijah prophets will love what God loves and hate what He hates.

We need to focus on the truth of the Word—not on being relevant or politically correct or making sure we don't offend any of our followers on social media. Sometimes we are so focused on being "relevant" that we end up being profane. We need to stay right in the middle of truth rather than dancing as close as we can to the edge of sin. God has called us to righteousness. He has called us to holiness. He has called us to be set apart. He has called us to be His own special people, chosen before the foundation of the world for good works so that we may walk in them.

While the primary *purpose* of the Elijah spirit is to turn hearts back to God, the primary *work* of the Elijah prophet is to bring revelation of God's character. When people truly understand who God is, how much He loves them, and how He wants to work in their lives, it softens hearts and draws people to the Lord.

The Elijah anointing challenges the motives of the religious. In Matthew 11, Jesus questioned the multitudes about John the Baptist (who operated in the spirit and power of Elijah and was the forerunner of Jesus):

> What did you go out into the wilderness to see? A reed shaken by the wind? But what did you go out to see? A man clothed in soft garments? Indeed, those who wear soft clothing are in kings' houses. But what did you go out to see? A prophet? Yes, I say to you, and more than a prophet. For this is he of whom it is written: "Behold,

I send My messenger before Your face, who will prepare
Your way before You."
—Matthew 11:7–10

Jesus knew that many people had gone to see John the
Baptist not out of sincere faith or hunger after the things of
God but rather out of a sense of religious superiority. They
weren't seeking truth; they were seeking to judge and condemn.
They went with a preconceived notion of what was right, and
their only purpose was to criticize. Their hearts were hard, as
often happens when people are caught up in religion rather
than having an intimate relationship with Jesus.

The Elijah anointing refuses to dance to the music of society's expectations. It is not child's play, and it transcends religious formalism—churches of compromise and temples of
tolerance—preaches righteousness, and repairs broken altars of
worship. Jesus said, "But to what shall I liken this generation?
It is like children sitting in the marketplaces and calling to
their companions, and saying: 'We played the flute for you,
and you did not dance; we mourned to you, and you did not
lament'" (Matt. 11:16–17).

The Elijah anointing comes from a place of maturity. It is
not going to dance to anyone else's music. It comes purely from
the heart of God. Those with the spirit of Elijah live to preach
messages that produce righteousness. They won't be part of a
religious system. They will purely speak the truth. They aren't
focused on preaching a beautiful, eloquent, perfectly worded
message. They bring the raw truth of God's Word. There is
no pretention. They believe what they preach, and they preach
what they believe.

The Elijah anointing has the nonreligious style of John the
Baptist. It is confrontational and challenging. It confronts all
illegal authority and puts us face-to-face with the truth. It
offends natural thinking, creating conflict and tension and

increasing our desperation to seek after and press into the heart of God. It is violent in how it opposes the human status quo. It is violent because it is disruptive; it is confrontational. Jesus said, "And from the days of John the Baptist until now the kingdom of heaven suffers violence, and the violent take it by force" (Matt. 11:12).

The Elijah anointing is relentless. It won't turn back, it won't waver, and it won't turn to the left or the right. It is in your face. The Elijah anointing doesn't have to be loud. It is the truth of God that confronts. It is resolved and obstinate against unrighteousness and wickedness. It doesn't back down or back up. It won't be silenced. It is spiritual warfare against deception about the ways of God.

If the Elijah anointing is at work in your life, you need to speak the truth with courage and boldness. Don't be afraid to offend anyone by speaking the truth of the Word because many, even within the church, are deceived. They have let the culture and their own offense lead them down wrong paths. They sit in church and hear, but they don't listen. The Word doesn't make it from their ears into their hearts. The Word doesn't prompt them to make changes in their lives. The Word doesn't move them to action. And because of that, they are deceiving themselves, just as the Bible warns: "But be doers of the word, and not hearers only, deceiving yourselves" (Jas. 1:22).

The spirit and power of Elijah is a miraculous ministry, operating in miracles, signs, and wonders and carrying the authority to govern the heavens. It fulfills the prophecy of Malachi 4:5–6 by turning hearts back to God. It is a fathering spirit that confronts the fatherlessness in our generation, sets the lonely in families, and calls the generations back to their identity and destiny in the kingdom of God. It is sustained by prayer and fasting and powered by Holy Spirit unction. And it comes to restore the roar and boldness back to the church.

THREE MOVEMENTS OF THE ELIJAH SPIRIT

There are three movements the Elijah spirit takes the people of God through to turn their hearts back to the Lord and restore their relationships with Him: revival, reformation, and restoration.

Revival

Revival refers to the act of being revived, of returning to life, of flourishing or becoming active again. When people turn away from the Lord, their faith is dead. Their spiritual lives are empty and barren. When people are in that state, they need revival. The Hebrew word for *revive* is *ḥāyâ*. It means to live; have life; to be restored to life or health; to revive from sickness, discouragement, faintness, or death; to give life; to nourish; to be whole.[5]

The psalmist Asaph wrote, "Return, we beseech You, O God of hosts; look down from heaven and see....Then we will not turn back from You; *revive* us, and we will call upon Your name" (Ps. 80:14, 18, emphasis added). Asaph recognized that in a time when people had turned away from the Lord, they needed to be revived. Psalm 119 declares what will bring about revival in the hearts of God's people—His Word: *"Revive* me according to Your word"* (v. 25, emphasis added).

The Elijah anointing emerges as a transformative force, poised to ignite a revival of unprecedented magnitude. Just as the prophet Elijah called down fire from heaven to purify and rekindle the hearts of the people, this anointing carries the potential to incite a spiritual fire that will cleanse, renew, and awaken the modern church.

In an era marked by distractions and worldly influences, the Elijah anointing will empower leaders and believers to boldly confront complacency and compromise, drawing them back to a fervent devotion to God's truth. It will embolden individuals to speak with prophetic authority, addressing societal issues with a clear moral compass and inspiring a hunger for righteousness.

Through passionate worship, fervent prayer, and an unwavering commitment to the Word of God, the Elijah anointing will not only restore the hearts of believers but also resonate beyond the church walls, drawing the lost into a life-transforming encounter with the living God. As this anointing sweeps across the twenty-first-century church, it carries the promise of revival, setting ablaze a renewed passion for God's kingdom and paving the way for a spiritual awakening that touches every corner of the world.

True revival requires repentance. To repent means to turn away from sin. It's not just slightly changing your direction—it's doing a complete one-eighty. The Hebrew word for *repent* is *šûb*, and it literally means to turn back; to retreat, deliver, draw back, rescue, relieve, restore, and return.[6] Repentance is the first step in being restored to a right relationship with the Lord.

When Elijah was on Mount Carmel, he asked the key question of the children of Israel: "How long will you falter between two opinions? If the LORD is God, follow Him; but if Baal, follow him" (1 Kings 18:21). Initially the people of Israel didn't respond to him at all. But when the time came for the showdown on Mount Carmel to reach its climax, Elijah declared, "LORD God of Abraham, Isaac, and Israel, let it be known this day that You are God in Israel and I am Your servant, and that I have done all these things at Your word. Hear me, O LORD, hear me, that this people may know that You are the LORD God, and that You have turned their hearts back to You again" (vv. 36–37).

Then the fire of the Lord fell from heaven.

There was no doubt in the minds of the people about who the real God was. Elijah-type prophets will always challenge the allegiance of your heart. The people fell on their faces, saying, "The LORD, He is God! The LORD, He is God!" (v. 39). It was the moment of repentance and the start of Israel's revival.

Reformation

Reformation is about correction, deliverance, and instruction. It is about tearing down the false altars people have built in their lives and redefining what is truth based on what God says in His Word rather than what the world says is true, or even an individual's "truth" about the world.

Elijah had to rebuild the altars of worship to the one true God once he tore down the altars to false gods. Remember, it isn't enough to just get rid of the false altars. It isn't enough to just tear down your idols. You need to replace them with truth; you need to replace them with worship of the Lord God Almighty. Make sure that Jesus is the One enthroned in your heart and mind, because if you don't you'll just end up with false altars and idols again. Don't just get rid of the lies; replace the lies with the truth.

Reformation is about a new commitment to holiness. Psalm 119 says:

> I have declared my ways, and You answered me; teach me Your statutes. Make me understand the way of Your precepts; so shall I meditate on Your wonderful works. My soul melts from heaviness; strengthen me according to Your word. Remove from me the way of lying, and grant me Your law graciously. I have chosen the way of truth.
>
> —Psalm 119:26–30

Revival leads to reformation. We need to know the truth. We need to know what the Word says about how to live. We need to know the precepts of the Lord. There is so much apostasy in the church because of lack of teaching on the basics of Scripture—what it means to be holy and set apart for the Lord. People are deconstructing the faith and falling away, so we need Elijahs to call people back to holiness and purity. Reformation is a call to hunger and thirst for righteousness, for when you do you will be filled.

13

Remember the key question Elijah asked: "How long will you falter between two opinions?" It's time to stop faltering. It's time to stand up and say, "As for me and my house, we will serve the Lord." It's time to tear down the false altars and root out the idols in our hearts and worship the one true God.

Restoration

Revival leads to reformation, which in turn leads to restoration. But in order for true restoration to occur, God's children must turn back to Him: "Turn us back to You, O LORD, and we will be restored" (Lam. 5:21). That is why a key part of the spirit of Elijah is turning hearts back to the Lord. Jesus Himself spoke of the restoration aspect of the spirit of Elijah: "Jesus answered and said to them, 'Indeed, Elijah is coming first and will restore all things'" (Matt. 17:11).

At the time, the disciples understood that Jesus was speaking about John the Baptist, the forerunner of the first coming of the Lord. But just as John the Baptist brought restoration in preparation for the first coming, I believe those with the spirit and power of Elijah today are called to bring restoration to those who have fallen away from the Lord, in preparation for the second coming.

Restoration is about restoring people in every way—spiritually, physically, mentally, emotionally, financially, and so forth. Restoration is about healing, rebuilding communities both in the church and outside of it, and restoring people's hope in the Lord. People need hope, but their hope needs to be in something real, something true. Romans 5:5 says, "Now hope does not disappoint, because the love of God has been poured out in our hearts by the Holy Spirit who was given to us."

Yes, Elijah called down fire, but the purpose was to get people to understand that the Lord is the true and living God. And when you understand that Jesus is Lord and there is no other, it brings hope. Jesus Christ is our living hope.

The prophecy about Elijah in the Book of Malachi says, "Behold, I will send you Elijah the prophet before the coming of the great and dreadful day of the LORD. And he will turn the hearts of the fathers to the children, and the hearts of the children to their fathers" (4:5–6). The turning of hearts back to the heavenly Father is a vital part of the Elijah anointing, but restoration of earthly families is a key component as well. The Father wants to bring us back into alignment with His plans and purposes as families.

The enemy of our souls has been destroying families right and left. Fatherlessness is at epidemic levels. We are living in a fatherless generation, and it is part of an epic battle for the souls of our children. While many mothers do a wonderful job raising their children as single parents, children still need fathers. We need fathers to be restored to their families, and we need spiritual fathers restored into the house of God.

So many people grew up without fathers, or they grew up with fathers who hurt, mistreated, or abused them. But the spirit of Elijah comes to bring restoration. It comes to heal families or to fill in the father gap in other ways. The Word says that God is a father to the fatherless (Ps. 68:5). It says, "God sets the solitary in families" (v. 6). God doesn't want to restore only individuals; He wants to restore families too. It is all part of the spirit of Elijah at work in the world.

WHAT ABOUT YOU?

As you awake to God's call to be an Elijah in this hour, His hand will rest on your life. You may have begun to feel a stirring and a zeal for the things of God in ways you never felt before. If this is so, pray, "Lord, let Your hand rest upon my life." His hand will bring security, stability, blessing, and favor into your life.

> For I, the LORD your God, hold your right hand; it is I
> who say to you, "Fear not, I am the one who helps you."
> —ISAIAH 41:13, ESV

You may feel alone, just as Elijah did, but God reminds you today that there are more like you who desire to serve Him. He reminds you today that He is with you. He will never leave you nor forsake you (Heb. 13:5). When the Creator of the heavens and the earth becomes your partner, all things are possible (Matt. 19:26). Limitations are broken when the hand of the Lord is upon you. When the hand of the Lord came upon Elijah, he outran the chariots of Ahab!

Chariots represent something of great power and speed. Chariots are also man-made. When the hand of the Lord is upon your life, you will overcome every man-made system or structure designed to stop you and prevent you from fulfilling your destiny. When the hand of the Lord comes upon you, there is an anointing of stamina and endurance released into your life. You may feel left behind or overwhelmed. But instead of falling prey to your feelings, decree that the hand of the Lord is supernaturally strengthening your life. Let endurance rest upon your soul. With the power of the Lord working in and through you, you have the ability to finish your course with joy!

The hand of God represents supernatural empowerment and might, and it is the impetus or force that will cause you to do great exploits for the Lord. Miracles, signs, and wonders will begin to flow into your life. When the hand of God comes upon you, a new authority and power comes that will enable you to destroy the enemies of your destiny.

> Your right hand, O LORD, glorious in power, your right
> hand, O LORD, shatters the enemy.
> —EXODUS 15:6, ESV

These are perilous times, but I want you to decree that even now the hand of Lord will touch your life. Let His power come upon you so that you will do great exploits for the kingdom, just as Elijah did in his day. Rise up in the spirit of boldness and declare that every enemy that comes to steal your heart and the heart of those to whom you are sent is destroyed! Let them know, "Elijah is here!"

PRAYER

May the spirit and power of Elijah sweep across our land, stirring hearts to repentance and reconciliation. Let the spirit of Elijah ignite a fire of love and unity within families, restoring broken relationships and nurturing compassion among generations.

In the wilderness of our lives, raise a voice, O Lord, in the spirit and power of Elijah, proclaiming the dawn of a new era. Prepare our hearts and minds for transformation, guiding us toward a higher purpose and a deeper connection with You.

Unleash miracles and signs through those anointed with the spirit and power of Elijah. Revive our faith, and restore hope in the hearts of the disheartened. Let these divine interventions be a testament to Your power and love, drawing us closer to You.

Grant us the courage to confront corruption and injustice, O Lord. May the spirit and power of Elijah embolden us to speak truth to power, challenge oppressive systems, and advocate for righteousness and accountability.

We declare the awakening of prophets anointed with the spirit and power of Elijah. By the authority of Your name, we release Your divine anointing upon these chosen vessels, igniting a fire within them to boldly proclaim Your truth.

In the mighty name of Jesus, we declare that these prophets rise up with a burning passion for righteousness and justice. They shall fearlessly confront the darkness that pervades our world, releasing Your brilliant light into every realm of despair.

By the power of the Holy Spirit, we declare an out-pouring of supernatural discernment and wisdom upon these prophets. They shall navigate this complex age with divine insight, guided by Your voice and walking in the path of Your divine purpose.

Father, we decree that their hearts be tender and compassionate, attuned to the cries of the broken and oppressed. They are agents of Your healing and restoration, advocates for the marginalized, and catalysts for divine justice in every situation.

In the spirit and power of Elijah, we declare that signs and wonders accompany their ministry. Miracles shall manifest as they boldly declare Your word, confirming its truth with undeniable supernatural demonstrations that captivate multitudes and draw them into Your loving embrace.

Lord, You are the giver of gifts, and we align ourselves to support and uplift these prophets. We stand in unwavering solidarity with them as they engage in spiritual battles, knowing that victory is assured through Your mighty hand.

By Your divine wisdom, I proclaim the rising of prophets who carry the spirit and power of Elijah in this generation. Their voices shall resound like thunder, penetrating through the noise and leading multitudes back to You. Revival will be sparked in hearts and nations as Your kingdom manifests in unprecedented ways.

We speak this declaration with unshakeable faith, knowing that You are faithful to fulfill Your promises. Let Your will be done, and may Your kingdom reign on earth as it does in heaven. In the mighty and matchless name of Jesus, we declare this to be so.

Chapter 2

When the Foundations
Are Destroyed

I BELIEVE WITHOUT A doubt that God is equipping a new generation of prophets with the spirit and power of Elijah. Their major assignment will be to challenge the moral decline and apostasy in the church. The theological drifts and doctrinal deviations within the church are alarming. The pressures of secularism, cultural inclusivity, and the desire to be relevant have led to a departure from essential truths and a watering down of biblical teachings. This departure weakens the church's foundation and undermines its ability to proclaim the fullness of God's truth.

Centuries ago the psalmist asked, "If the foundations be destroyed, what can the righteous do?" (Ps. 11:3, KJV). This question must be answered by this generation of leaders. My response is found in Ephesians 2:20: we must recognize and build upon the foundation of the apostles and prophets, with Christ as the chief cornerstone. Just as the cornerstone determines the alignment and stability of a building, today's leaders must recognize Jesus Christ as the supreme authority and foundation upon which all aspects of ministry and leadership are built. Modern-day Elijah prophets are needed to build and strengthen the foundation of the church.

The transformative power that marked the prophet Elijah is needed in the present age. The church needs boldness, prophetic conviction, and a resolute commitment to righteousness. Elijah's example inspires repentance, revival, and a renewed pursuit of God's truth. By challenging cultural influences and apostasy, the church can reclaim its identity as a beacon of light in a dark world. With faith and dependence on God, the church can experience a revival of spiritual vitality and witness the transformative power of modern-day Elijahs, operating under the anointing of the Holy Spirit, at work in our midst.

The emergence of modern-day prophets anointed with the spirit and power of Elijah is a testament to God's faithfulness in every generation. These chosen vessels possess a prophetic calling that transcends cultural norms and societal expectations. They embody distinctive characteristics that reflect their unwavering commitment to truth and righteousness, and their spiritual gifts enable them to confront moral decay, apostasy, and spiritual complacency.

As we witness the rise of these anointed prophets, let us embrace their ministry and receive their words with humility and discernment. May we recognize their calling as a divine gift to the church, provoking us to examine our lives, align with God's truth, and fervently pursue revival. Through their anointing, the spirit and power of Elijah will flow, igniting a holy fire within our hearts and ushering in a transformation that will shape the course of history.

God is mantling Elijah-type prophets to confront the increasing apostasy and theological drift within the church. Apostasy refers to the abandonment of core Christian beliefs and practices. Theological drift occurs when the church departs from sound biblical doctrine, embracing teachings that dilute or distort the gospel. The pressures of secularism, cultural inclusivity, and the desire to be relevant have led to a departure from essential truths and a watering down of biblical teachings. This departure weakens the church's foundation and undermines its ability to proclaim the fullness of God's truth.

In his book *Why So Many Christians Have Left the Faith*, Dr. Michael Brown states that a compromised gospel message produces compromised fruit. Today we preach all kinds of other gospels, messages mixed with enough truth to resemble the real gospel but not enough truth to convert and transform; messages with enough Scripture to sound right but mingled with enough poison to kill.

What are some of these complex messages prevalent today?

- The health and prosperity gospel, luring with promises of physical healing and boundless financial success upon the condition of one's belief.

- The motivational discourse gospel, where the preacher takes on the role of a life mentor, aiming to saturate you with positivity, feelings of contentment, and accomplishments.

- The gospel of celebrity, which essentially suggests, "Observe all these renowned and appealing figures who align themselves with Christ. Is not that allure enticing?"

- The progressive gospel, portraying Jesus as an enlightened teacher now attuned to the values of the contemporary world.

- The gospel of social justice, predominantly sim-
  plifying multifaceted topics to matters of race
  and justice, with Jesus seen as a remedy for
  societal injustices rather than a means of reconciling us to God.

Such a manner of preaching has the potential to undermine the very foundations of the church. When these mixed
messages, though seemingly infused with elements of truth,
are allowed to permeate, they erode the core tenets of the faith
upon which the church stands. The distortion of gospel truths,
the dilution of Scripture's authenticity, and the manipulation
of divine principles ultimately weaken the spiritual fabric the
church is built upon.

The resulting confusion, disillusionment, and compromised
beliefs can lead to a fragmentation of the church's unity and a
departure from the essential truths that have anchored believers for generations. Therefore, it is paramount to guard against
these tendencies and strive for preaching that upholds the
unadulterated Word, ensuring the preservation of the church's
foundations and the spiritual vitality of its members.

The spirit and power of Elijah counteract increasing apostasy and theological drift by upholding sound doctrine and
faithfully proclaiming the fullness of God's truth. Elijah stood
firmly against the prophets of Baal, exposing their false teachings and leading the people back to the worship of the true
God.

In the same manner, modern-day prophets equipped with
the spirit and power of Elijah can confront apostasy and
theological drift by proclaiming the uncompromised gospel
message. They can expose false teachings, challenge distorted
interpretations of Scripture, and point believers back to the
unchanging truths of God's Word. Prophets anointed with the

spirit and power of Elijah stand as unwavering beacons of absolute truth in a sea of moral relativism.

Modern-day Elijahs are poised to play a pivotal role in restoring the foundations that have been eroded within the church. Just as the original Elijah confronted idolatry and brought about a renewal of faith, these contemporary spiritual leaders are called to stand as beacons of truth and restoration.

These Elijahs are not mere spectators but active participants in rebuilding the spiritual infrastructure. Through their teaching, mentorship, and example, they guide believers to rediscover the depth of Scripture, reestablishing a solid connection to the authentic teachings of Christ. Their emphasis on uncompromised doctrine and righteous living acts as a catalyst for revival, breathing life back into the church's foundation.

As they boldly confront societal pressures and cultural influences that threaten the integrity of faith, modern-day Elijahs inspire a return to the core principles of the gospel. Their dedication to prayer, discernment, and unwavering conviction propels believers to anchor themselves in the unchanging truths of Scripture.

In essence, these spiritual leaders carry the mantle of Elijah, not only identifying the crumbling foundations but actively participating in their restoration. Through their efforts, they pave the way for a revitalized church that stands firm on the unshakeable foundation of God's Word, ready to impact the world with renewed strength and purpose.

Through these modern-day Elijah prophets, the church can grow in its understanding of the prophetic calling, the importance of discernment, and the pursuit of personal and corporate revival. Ultimately, the goal is to align with God's purposes, bring transformation to individuals and communities, and advance the kingdom of God. We must return to a gospel that humbles us, convicts us, warns us, saves us, and causes us to grieve for our own sin as well as the sin of others.

The modern-day Elijahs of God will rise to the occasion, summoning leaders to emulate the fervor of the historical Elijah, with a passion ablaze for God's glory and a profound concern for the welfare of their nation. Like the prophet of old, these contemporary Elijahs will beckon leaders to transcend personal agendas and ambitions and prioritize the honor and splendor of God above all, fueling their actions with unwavering devotion to the betterment of their people. They will encourage leaders to be instruments of God's solutions for the challenges facing their communities, fostering an environment where God's will is not just known but fully embraced.

Ultimately, the modern-day Elijahs will galvanize leaders to be catalysts of change, driven by an unquenchable fire for God's glory and a burning concern for the well-being of their nations. Through their unwavering devotion, they will lead leaders into a transformative journey of availability, where they become instruments in the hands of God, agents of change, and champions of His redemptive plan.

THE SNARE OF TOLERANCE

Tolerance is a word we hear often. It is generally spoken of as a virtue. No one wants to be labeled as intolerant in this day and age.

Merriam-Webster defines *tolerance* as "sympathy or indulgence for beliefs or practices differing from or conflicting with one's own; the act of allowing something."[3] Dictionary. com defines it as "a fair, respectful, and permissive attitude or policy toward people whose opinions, beliefs, practices, racial or ethnic origins, etc., differ from one's own or from those of the majority; freedom from bigotry and from an insistence on conformity."[4]

Those definitions of tolerance make it sound like a really good thing. And the truth is that biblical tolerance is a good thing. If we define *tolerance* as treating others with love, kindness, and respect, even when we disagree with them, tolerance is a biblical virtue. The apostle Paul wrote, "I...beseech you to walk worthy of the calling with which you were called, with all lowliness and gentleness, with longsuffering, bearing with one another in love, endeavoring to keep the unity of the Spirit in the bond of peace" (Eph. 4:1–3). One translation of Ephesians 4:2 says, "...showing tolerance for one another in love" (NASB).

In reference to dealing with others, the Bible also says:

> Finally, all of you be of one mind, having compassion for one another; love as brothers, be tenderhearted, be courteous; not returning evil for evil or reviling for reviling, but on the contrary blessing, knowing that you were called to this, that you may inherit a blessing.
> —1 PETER 3:8–9

Love, mercy, compassion, respect, and doing good to others are all wrapped up in the traditional understanding of tolerance. But the definition of *tolerance* has been changing. Tolerance is no longer just about respecting the right of others to have opinions that are different from yours. Tolerance now means you have to accept all opinions and perspectives and lifestyles and "truths" as equally valid. That is where the problem lies.

Tolerance now means there is no absolute truth. It says there are no black-and-white standards. People are free to decide for themselves what they think is true or acceptable. If a person thinks something is OK, then it must be OK—if you say otherwise, you are being intolerant. The Bible may say that adultery is a sin, but if someone thinks it is acceptable according to their "truth," then adultery isn't a sin anymore. And not only that, if you say adultery is a sin, you are being intolerant.

Tolerance means you are expected to give blind approval to whatever someone else says is right or true or good—no matter what it is. Not too long ago almost everyone would have said

25

that marriage is between one man and one woman, but in the times we are living in, if you say marriage is between one man and one woman, you are being intolerant. You can say, "Well, the Bible says, 'Therefore a man shall leave his father and mother and be joined to his wife, and they shall become one flesh,' so that seems to be a pretty clear indication that God defines marriage as being between one man and one woman," but it doesn't matter (Gen. 2:24). Society has succumbed to the homosexual agenda and dismissed the truth of the Word of God about marriage.

However, when you dismiss the truth of God's Word, or when you cherry-pick what you think is true from the Word of God, you are on a slippery slope. You are putting yourself in danger because you are removing yourself from a solid foundation. Relative truth is dangerous because there are no absolutes. When you don't have black-and-white standards for truth and morality, the line between good and evil starts to move. And with Satan being the ruler of this world for now, the line does not move in a good direction.

Another issue with society's current understanding of tolerance is that tolerance is the end goal. People want to be free to believe and do whatever they want—with no judgment, no consequences, no repercussions, no accountability, and no regard for the well-being of others. But tolerance is not the end goal of biblical tolerance, nor does biblical tolerance mean people have a free pass to do whatever they want. The Word says, "God's kindness is meant to lead you to repentance" (Rom. 2:4, esv). So we need to have compassion for the lost, and we need to have the desire to see them saved, delivered, and set free. That means while we treat them with respect, mercy, and love, we also share the truth with boldness and in love, for the Lord is "not willing that any should perish but that all should come to repentance" (2 Pet. 3:9).

If we adhere to society's understanding of tolerance, people will not recognize their sin and their need of the Savior. The apostle Paul wrote that "whoever calls on the name of the LORD shall be saved." But he followed that statement by asking, "How then shall they call on Him in whom they have not believed? And how shall they believe in Him of whom they have not heard?" (Rom. 10:13–14).

The world's definition of tolerance silences believers. It keeps them from sharing the gospel. It keeps them from reaching out to hurting, broken people in bondage to sin with the truth that will heal them, give them hope, and set them free. The Lord paid a high price to set everyone free from their sin. How can we let "tolerance" condemn so many of the lost to hell because we allowed ourselves to be muzzled? That is not the heart of the Lord.

And let's also be clear: Jesus was intolerant of many things. Jesus didn't say all paths lead to heaven or that there are many ways to salvation. He said, "I am the way, the truth, and the life. No one comes to the Father except through Me" (John 14:6), and, "Enter by the narrow gate; for wide is the gate and broad is the way that leads to destruction, and there are many who go in by it" (Matt. 7:13).

Jesus was also intolerant of sin. He was tolerant of sinners, but He was intolerant toward the sin that kept them in bondage. Take the woman caught in adultery, for example. He didn't condemn her. He didn't cast stones at her, demean her, ridicule her, or belittle her. He told her, "Go and sin no more" (John 8:11).

So while biblical tolerance is a way to help us reach the lost, worldly tolerance only leads to compromise and destruction. Biblical tolerance leads to freedom in Christ, hope, and peace; worldly tolerance leads to bondage, despair, and turmoil. To operate in the spirit and power of Elijah, we cannot allow ourselves to be silenced by the fear of being labeled intolerant. We need to open our mouths and speak the truth of the Word of

God. We need to be voices crying out, calling people to repentance and to turn back to the Lord.

Tolerance, when taken to an extreme or misapplied, can lead to compromise within the church. It can be misinterpreted or distorted in a way that undermines biblical truth and dilutes the uncompromising message of the gospel. When tolerance becomes an absolute value without any discernment or boundaries, it can erode the firm foundation of the church. This can manifest in several ways:

Relativism—Excessive tolerance can lead to relativism, the belief that all perspectives and beliefs are equally valid and true. When this mindset infiltrates the church, it undermines the absolute truth of God's Word. It can lead to a watering down of biblical teachings, compromising the distinctiveness of the Christian faith.

Moral compromise—Unrestrained tolerance may encourage the acceptance of behaviors and practices that are contrary to the teachings of Scripture. It can erode moral standards and dilute the call to holiness. The church may feel pressured to compromise on issues such as sexual ethics, marriage, and the sanctity of life, undermining biblical values to accommodate societal expectations.

Doctrinal dilution—Overemphasis on tolerance can lead to a diminishing of doctrinal clarity. In an attempt to avoid disagreement or offense, essential theological truths may be downplayed or ignored. This can result in a loss of theological distinctiveness and compromise on core doctrines of the Christian faith.

Spiritual apathy—When tolerance is wrongly equated with acceptance of all beliefs, it can lead to spiritual apathy and complacency. The urgency to

share the gospel and call people to repentance and
faith in Christ may diminish. The church may
become hesitant to speak truth boldly, fearing it
may offend or be seen as intolerant.

It is crucial to strike a balance between tolerance and unwavering commitment to biblical truth. The church is called to be loving, compassionate, and respectful toward others while remaining steadfast in the teachings and values outlined in Scripture. This requires discernment, wisdom, and a reliance on the Holy Spirit to navigate the complexities of a diverse world without compromising the unchanging truths of the gospel.

BREAKING THE SPIRIT OF RELIGION AND TRADITIONS OF MAN

The spirit and power of Elijah also comes to break the spirit of religion. The spirit of religion replaces the joy of a genuine, intimate relationship with the Lord with adhering to a bunch of dos and don'ts. Conforming to a set of rules and traditions replaces being transformed by the work of the Holy Spirit in your life. The religious spirit says you have to do certain things and serve God in certain ways to get His approval or to be blessed by Him. The religious spirit has no room for the grace of God. This spirit is about outward appearance rather than inward transformation and growth.

The prophet Isaiah described the religious spirit this way:

> These people draw near with their mouths and honor Me with their lips, but have removed their hearts far from Me, and their fear toward Me is taught by the commandment of men.
>
> —ISAIAH 29:13

People with a religious spirit give lip service to the Lord, but their hearts have turned from Him. They go through the motions of religious tradition—they go to church on Sunday mornings, pray before meals, have a few Bible verses they can quote in certain situations, and appear outwardly pious in every way. But they are really hypocrites because their piety is only skin deep. They are like the scribes and Pharisees in the New Testament. Jesus was anything but tolerant of their hypocrisy. He said:

> The scribes and the Pharisees sit in Moses' seat. Therefore whatever they tell you to observe, that observe and do, but do not do according to their works; for they say, and do not do. For they bind heavy burdens, hard to bear, and lay them on men's shoulders; but they themselves will not move them with one of their fingers. But all their works they do to be seen by men....
>
> But woe to you, scribes and Pharisees, hypocrites! For you shut up the kingdom of heaven against men; for you neither go in yourselves, nor do you allow those who are entering to go in. Woe to you, scribes and Pharisees, hypocrites! For you devour widows' houses, and for a pretense make long prayers. Therefore you will receive greater condemnation....
>
> Woe to you, scribes and Pharisees, hypocrites! For you pay tithe of mint and anise and cummin, and have neglected the weightier matters of the law: justice and mercy and faith. These you ought to have done, without leaving the others undone. Blind guides, who strain out a gnat and swallow a camel!
>
> Woe to you, scribes and Pharisees, hypocrites! For you cleanse the outside of the cup and dish, but inside they are full of extortion and self-indulgence. Blind Pharisee, first cleanse the inside of the cup and dish, that the outside of them may be clean also.
>
> Woe to you, scribes and Pharisees, hypocrites! For you

are like whitewashed tombs which indeed appear beautiful outwardly, but inside are full of dead men's bones
and all uncleanness. Even so you also outwardly appear
righteous to men, but inside you are full of hypocrisy
and lawlessness.

—MATTHEW 23:1–5, 13–14, 23–28

The Lord doesn't want lip service. He doesn't want you to
do good works out of a sense of obligation or to try to earn
His blessing. He wants your heart. He wants you to obey and
serve Him with joy out of love, not out of a sense of duty or
tradition. He doesn't want you putting on a mask of righteousness while your heart is hard and full of sin. He wants to clean
you up from the inside out. He is the only One who can do
it. You can't clean yourself up. Jesus is the only One who can
cleanse you and make you whole. And He longs to do that for
you. First John 1:9 says, "If we confess our sins, He is faithful and just to forgive us our sins and to cleanse us from all
unrighteousness."

The spirit of religion and the traditions of men are traps.
They keep us from having a genuine relationship with the
Lord. During the days of Elijah, many of the Israelites were
caught in the trap of religion and tradition. Remember, even
though they bore the name of God in the name of their nation
(*el* means God), when it really came down to it, they had just
been going through the motions. When Elijah posed the key
question on Mount Carmel, "How long will you falter between
two opinions?" the people of Israel just looked at him (1 Kings
18:21). They didn't say a word. In turning away from the Lord,
they ended up with religion rather than relationship. Their
faith ended up a farce.

But the spirit and power of Elijah comes to shake people out
of their religious stupor. It comes to wake up people who have
been sleepwalking, adhering only to man-made traditions and

not pursuing a genuine relationship with the Lord. The spirit and power of Elijah comes to turn the hearts of people back to the Lord and renew their passion for Him. The Elijah anointing preaches the truth of the Word with power and sets people on fire for the Lord of hosts. There is then no doubt that "the LORD, He is God! The Lord, He is God!" (1 Kings 18:39).

IF THE LORD IS GOD...

In the midst of the showdown on Mount Carmel with the prophets of Baal, after he asked the people the key question, "How long will you falter between two opinions?," the prophet Elijah followed up with a challenge: "If the LORD is God, follow Him; but if Baal, follow him" (1 Kings 18:21). He was challenging the people about their idols.

During the days of Elijah, there were clear idols, or false gods, that the people chose to follow and worship. Baal was the most common, but they also worshipped other false gods, such as Asherah, Astarte, and Molech. The worship of these gods included child sacrifice, especially to Molech, and sexual promiscuity, among other things.

Leviticus 18:21 specifically forbids the people of Israel from making their children "pass through the fire to Molech." Child sacrifice to Molech involved placing a child in the outstretched arms of a statue of the deity with an oven inside; the child would be burned alive while music played to drown out the child's cries. The sacrifice of innocent children was and is an abomination to the Lord, and it breaks His heart. Proverbs 6:16–17 says, "These six things the LORD hates, yes, seven are an abomination to Him: a proud look, a lying tongue, hands that shed innocent blood."

We don't worship Molech today, and we don't practice child sacrifice the way some ancient cultures did. Yet many hands have shed innocent blood by means of abortion, and abortion has become an idol in the hearts of many.

An idol is anything that gets first place in your heart instead of the Lord. People may not worship Baal or Astarte anymore, but they still are guilty of idolatry. The idols we have today look different. They aren't statues made of wood or bronze. Instead they are things such as money, sex, identity, social status, entertainment, personal comfort, relationships, science, sports, pornography, and so forth. The things we turn into idols aren't always necessarily bad things in and of themselves. Money is a good thing, but the love of money isn't. Sex is a good thing, but God created it and intended it for a man and woman to enjoy within the bond of marriage. Loving your spouse and your children is also a good thing. But when any of these things takes first place in your heart, it becomes idolatry. An idol is anything that steals away the affections of God's people.

The Bible has a lot to say about idolatry:

> You shall have no other gods before Me.
>
> —EXODUS 20:3

> Therefore put to death your members which are on the earth: fornication, uncleanness, passion, evil desire, and covetousness, which is idolatry.
>
> —COLOSSIANS 3:5

> Their land is also full of idols; they worship the work of their own hands.
>
> —ISAIAH 2:8

> These men have set up their idols in their hearts, and put before them that which causes them to stumble into iniquity.
>
> —EZEKIEL 14:3

> They served their idols, which became a snare to them.
>
> —PSALM 106:36

The point is that idols are a trap, a snare. They draw us away from the Lord and into sin. Idols lock away our hearts. The Elijah anointing proclaims the vengeance of God on idolatry. God has always wanted a people who voluntarily love and worship Him. Idolatry robs God of His desire, but because of His great love for us He will literally move heaven and earth to bring us back to Him. That is why in this season of great idolatry—when so many have turned away from the Lord to worship money, sex, themselves, or other idols—the Lord is sending prophets in the spirit and power of Elijah. He is sending prophets to challenge the people of God about whom they are really serving and worshipping.

It is time for the hearts of God's people to be turned back to Him. It is time for modern-day Elijahs to stand up, boldly proclaim the truth, speak out against the spirit of religion and the traditions of man, and challenge people about their idolatry. It is time for voices to be heard in the wilderness, preparing the way for the second coming of the Lord.

Chapter 3

The Making of an Elijah

THE FIRST MENTION of the prophet Elijah in the Bible is in 1 Kings:

> And Elijah the Tishbite, of the inhabitants of Gilead, said to Ahab, "As the LORD God of Israel lives, before whom I stand, there shall not be dew nor rain these years, except at my word."
>
> —1 KINGS 17:1

Elijah's first assignment involved judgment. In a land consumed by idolatry and iniquity, he was given the job of decreeing the judgment of God. Elijah decreed that there would be a drought in the land, and there was. Because the people of Israel had to grow their own food, a drought didn't just mean you couldn't water your lawn. It meant your crops wouldn't grow. It meant there would be no grain to harvest, no grapes and olives to pick. It meant that your livestock would die from lack of water and food. It meant famine. It meant suffering. It meant death. But the thing is that Elijah lived in the land too. The drought would not just bring suffering to the idolaters but also to Elijah and any others in the land who were still following the one true God.

When you are a prophet of God and God gives you a judgment to decree over a certain region within which you dwell, you need to be prepared to suffer too. God gave Elijah a powerful judgment for Israel—that rain would not fall on their land and they would suffer from drought and famine because they refused to worship God and worshipped the idols of Baal and Asherah instead. Elijah came to realize this truth immediately: you can't divorce yourself from the prophecies God commands you to deliver. Yet Elijah also discovered that the Lord will hide you away and cover you in those times of suffering.

HIDDEN WITH GOD

When the drought began, the Lord had a plan for Elijah.

> Then the word of the LORD came to him, saying, "Get away from here and turn eastward, and hide by the Brook Cherith, which flows into the Jordan. And it will be that you shall drink from the brook, and I have commanded the ravens to feed you there." So he went and did according to the word of the LORD, for he went and stayed by the Brook Cherith, which flows into the Jordan. The ravens brought him bread and meat in the morning, and bread and meat in the evening; and he drank from the brook.
>
> —1 KINGS 17:2–6

It wasn't time for Elijah to confront Ahab yet, so the Lord hid him away. He sent Elijah to a place of safety and provided for his needs. It was also an opportunity for Elijah to spend time with the Lord and develop an even closer relationship with Him. It was a waiting time for Elijah.

Times of waiting happen for all of us. But if we are wise, we will make use of those times of waiting. During the waiting time, we need to continue growing and serving the Lord. And the waiting time makes us strong.

Isaiah 40:31 says, "But those who wait on the LORD shall renew their strength; they shall mount up with wings like eagles, they shall run and not be weary, they shall walk and not faint." The word translated "wait" means to bind together, like twisting strands of a rope together.[1] When you are waiting, it is a time for you to be bound together with the Lord, for He is the source of your strength. When you spend your waiting time pursuing the Lord, He will give you the supernatural strength you need when the moment comes for you to step out and walk in the fullness of the spirit and power of Elijah. During this time of waiting, the Lord gives you His heart and mind for your calling. During this time at the Brook Cherith, He cuts away any human perspectives and perceptions. This is where God infuses you with His emotions and where the zeal for Him is birthed. Elijahs will confront unrighteousness and idol worship because they will love what God loves and hate what He hates.

The Lord sent Elijah to a brook, a source of water. When we are in the midst of a waiting time, we need water. We need to be refreshed. The Word says, "Times of refreshing...come from the presence of the Lord" (Acts 3:19). We need our thirst for the Lord and His righteousness to be filled. And the Lord promised, "Blessed are those who hunger and thirst for righteousness, for they shall be filled" (Matt. 5:6).

We also need to be cleansed. Psalm 51:7 says, "Purge me with hyssop, and I shall be clean; wash me, and I shall be whiter than snow." The Word of God is what washes us and cleanses us during the waiting times:

> Christ also loved the church and gave Himself for her, that
> He might sanctify and cleanse her with the washing of
> water by the word, that He might present her to Himself

37

a glorious church, not having spot or wrinkle or any such
thing, but that she should be holy and without blemish.

—EPHESIANS 5:25–27

When you are in a time of waiting, a time of being hidden
with God, you need to spend time in the Word, letting it
speak to you, change you, encourage you, strengthen you, and
prepare you.

There is something interesting about the Hebrew word for
brook. The word itself, *nahal*, means exactly what you would
expect: brook, stream, or river.[2] You might expect the root
word to have something to do with water, but it doesn't. The
root word is *nāhal*, and it means to inherit or to cause to
inherit.[3] When we are intentional and earnest in our pursuit
of the Lord, when our lives are hidden with Him, when we
are waiting patiently and being transformed by His Word and
the work of the Holy Spirit, we are partaking of our spiritual
inheritance. Acts 20:32 says, "I commend you to God and
to the word of His grace, which is able to build you up and
give you an inheritance among all those who are sanctified."
Ephesians 1:17–21 says:

...that the God of our Lord Jesus Christ, the Father of
glory, may give to you the spirit of wisdom and revelation in the knowledge of Him, the eyes of your understanding being enlightened; that you may know what
is the hope of His calling, what are the riches of the
glory of His inheritance in the saints, and what is the
exceeding greatness of His power toward us who believe,
according to the working of His mighty power which
He worked in Christ when He raised Him from the
dead and seated Him at His right hand in the heavenly
places, far above all principality and power and might
and dominion, and every name that is named, not only
in this age but also in that which is to come.

Our spiritual inheritance in the Lord is rooted in the Word. The Word of God strengthens us, encourages us, and builds us up. It sanctifies us and transforms us. It gives us wisdom, revelation, knowledge, and understanding that we need to walk in the spirit and power of Elijah. It gives us a preview of the power available to us when the time comes for our Mount Carmel showdown or for us to operate in miracles, signs, and wonders. It reminds us that God is greater than any principality or power that might come against us as we are walking in the fullness of God's plan for our lives. These are all key concepts that you need to meditate on during your waiting time—your time of being hidden with the Lord. It is a time for the Lord to equip you for what lies ahead.

The Lord didn't send Elijah to just any brook. He specifically sent Elijah to the Brook Cherith. The Hebrew word for Cherith is *kərîṯ*. It means cutting.[4] That means our time of being hidden with the Lord is a time for us to be changed. It is a time for the Lord to cut away things that are hindering us or getting in the way of how He wants to use us. It is a time for us to be transformed, to be changed from the inside out by the Lord. This is especially important for those walking in the spirit and power of Elijah. It is all too easy for us to fall into the trap of conforming to the ways of the world, to buy in to political correctness, to give in to the fear of man. But the Word says, "Do not be conformed to this world, but be transformed by the renewing of your mind, that you may prove what is that good and acceptable and perfect will of God" (Rom. 12:2). The Brook Cherith is a place of renewal and refreshing. It is a place of change.

Also take note that when Elijah went to the Brook Cherith, it was an act of obedience. Just because God has given you a gift, a calling, an assignment, and a message does not mean the time to act on them is now. To walk in the spirit and power of Elijah, you need to obey the voice of the Lord. You can't let pride get in the way. Jesus said, "You are My friends if you do whatever I command you" (John 15:14). If the Lord tells you to hide and wait, you need to hide and wait. And when He tells you it's time to go, you need to go. Obedience to the word of the Lord is critical for Elijahs.

The season of waiting and prayer at the Brook Cherith kept Elijah connected to the heart of God. When Elijah first spoke to Ahab, he described the Lord as the one "before whom I stand" (1 Kings 17:1). Elijah was boldly declaring both his allegiance to and the authority of the kingdom he represented. God uses this time of separation to purify your heart and motives. Elijah had already spent time in the presence of the Lord, and he boldly declared that to Ahab. But he needed more time in the presence of God. There is no substitute for time in the presence of the Lord. In His presence is fullness of joy (Ps. 16:11). His presence saves (Isa. 63:9). It refreshes (Acts 3:19). It moves mountains (Ps. 68:8, 97:5; Isa. 64:3).

The time Elijah spent in the presence of the Lord at the Brook Cherith was part of his growth process. He was learning to depend on the Lord to meet both his physical and spiritual needs. He was also developing the spirit of intercession and the prayer mantle so integral to the Elijah anointing. Remember, Elijah prayed that it wouldn't rain, and that is exactly what happened.

> The effective, fervent prayer of a righteous man avails much. Elijah was a man with a nature like ours, and he prayed earnestly that it would not rain; and it did not rain on the land for three years and six months. And he prayed again, and the heaven gave rain, and the earth produced its fruit.
>
> —JAMES 5:16–18

When the Lord hides you away for a season of waiting, don't get discouraged. Spend time in the presence of the Lord.

Bind yourself together with Him. Be refreshed, renewed, cleansed, transformed, changed, encouraged, and empowered. Dig into His Word—read it, meditate on it, pray it back to the Lord, write it on your heart, and get it into your spirit. Develop the spirit of intercession, and pray effective, fervent prayers. It is all part of preparing you for walking in the spirit and power of Elijah.

Hiddenness with God is often seen as a place of intimacy and encounter, where individuals experience God's presence, receive revelation, and deepen their trust and reliance on Him. It can be a time of spiritual refinement, where God works in the hidden places of our hearts, refining our motives, aligning our desires with His, and preparing us for the next steps in our journeys.

UNCONVENTIONAL PROVISION

When Elijah was hidden away at the Brook Cherith, the Lord provided for him. First Kings 17:6 tells us, "The ravens brought him bread and meat in the morning, and bread and meat in the evening; and he drank from the brook." Elijah had supernatural provision.

However, the supernatural provision was also unconventional. The ravens at the brook that fed Elijah represent God's unconventional method of provision for His Elijah prophets. God's provision doesn't always look like what we expect. We see that many times in the Word of God. For example, when the children of Israel were wandering in the wilderness after the exodus from Egypt, God fed them with manna. Manna was definitely not what they were expecting. In fact, the Hebrew word for *manna* means "What is it?"[5] They had no idea what manna was, and it was not what they expected God to provide—but it was exactly what they needed.

God chose to use ravens to provide food for Elijah at the brook. That was an interesting choice because ravens, along with other scavengers, are among the birds listed as unclean in the Law:

> And these you shall regard as an abomination among the birds; they shall not be eaten, they are an abomination: the eagle, the vulture, the buzzard, the kite, and the falcon after its kind; every raven after its kind, the ostrich, the short-eared owl, the sea gull, and the hawk after its kind; the little owl, the fisher owl, and the screech owl; the white owl, the jackdaw, and the carrion vulture; the stork, the heron after its kind, the hoopoe, and the bat.
>
> —Leviticus 11:13–19

Elijah being fed by a bird considered unclean reminds me of Peter's vision on a rooftop in Joppa:

> The next day, as they went on their journey and drew near the city, Peter went up on the housetop to pray, about the sixth hour. Then he became very hungry and wanted to eat; but while they made ready, he fell into a trance and saw heaven opened and an object like a great sheet bound at the four corners, descending to him and let down to the earth. In it were all kinds of four-footed animals of the earth, wild beasts, creeping things, and birds of the air. And a voice came to him, "Rise, Peter; kill and eat."
>
> But Peter said, "Not so, Lord! For I have never eaten anything common or unclean."
>
> And a voice spoke to him again the second time, "What God has cleansed you must not call common." This was done three times. And the object was taken up into heaven again.
>
> —Acts 10:9–16

Peter wondered what his vision meant, but it became clear when he was summoned to visit the home of a Gentile named Cornelius. As Peter talked with Cornelius as he arrived, "he went in and found many who had come together. Then he said to them, 'You know how unlawful it is for a Jewish man to keep company with or go to one of another nation. But God has shown me that I should not call any man common or unclean'" (Acts 10:27–28).

Peter used two adjectives: *common* and *unclean*. The Greek word for *common*, *koinos*, means common, defiled, unclean, and unholy, in the sense of being shared by many people.[6] The Greek word for *unclean*, *akathartos*, means foul, impure, unclean, or even demonic (e.g., unclean spirits).[7] All those words sum up the opinions that Jews, even followers of Jesus, often had of Gentiles.

Cornelius, even though he was a Gentile, was devout and feared the Lord. And he was hungry for the Word of the Lord, just as Peter and Elijah were hungry for food. When summoned by Cornelius, Peter had a choice: he could give in to prejudice and religious tradition and refuse to go, or he could follow the leading of the Lord, set his preconceived notions aside, and speak the truth to the one he was being called to.

Elijahs have the same choice. We often have prejudices and traditions that are so ingrained in us that we think we must be mistaken if God sends us to someone who doesn't meet our preconceived notions of the kind of people we should preach to, prophesy to, speak the truth to, minister to, or serve. When we think of prejudice, we often think of things like racism and sexism—and both of those are definitely prejudices that need to be rooted out of the hearts of those who want to walk in the spirit and power of Elijah. But there are others, some rooted in religious tradition and others rooted in the attitudes we have allowed into our own hearts.

As Elijahs, we need to be connected with the heart of the

Lord—and the Lord is "not willing that any should perish but that all should come to repentance" (2 Pet. 3:9). We can't let any prejudices, hang-ups, traditions, or preconceived notions get in the way. Some people may be hesitant to minister to a homeless person because of their physical condition. Some people may be hesitant to prophesy to a millionaire because they are intimidated by the person's wealth. Some people may be hesitant to speak truth to someone because of the color of their skin. Some people may not want to bother with people from certain denominations. Some people may not want to minister to prostitutes, drug addicts, law enforcement officers, elderly people, people with mental disabilities, people with physical disabilities... The list could go on and on.

But when God is calling you, it is not about what makes you comfortable. It is not about what you are used to. It is not about what you are familiar with. It is about being in tune with the Holy Spirit and following His lead. It is about not judging for yourself whether someone is worthy or willing to hear the word of the Lord. It is about obeying the Lord and reaching the lost—whoever that happens to be in your life. To walk in the spirit and power of Elijah, it is both necessary and important to follow the Lord wherever He leads—even when it means going out of bounds from what is normal for you.

THE VOICE OF ONE

The time at the Brook Cherith was Elijah's wilderness experience. Wilderness experiences consistently show up in Scripture as part of a prophet's development. After Moses killed the Egyptian, he fled to Midian and spent about forty years in the desert tending his father-in-law's sheep before the Lord appeared to him at the burning bush and called him to deliver the Israelites from bondage in Egypt. After Jesus was baptized, He was in the wilderness for forty days being tempted by the devil.

John the Baptist, who came in the spirit and power of Elijah as the forerunner of Jesus Christ's first coming, also had a wilderness experience. In fact, his entire life was pretty much a wilderness experience. Luke 1:80 says, "So the child [John] grew and became strong in spirit, and was in the deserts till the day of his manifestation to Israel."

Jewish men in the priestly tribe of Levi did not begin their ministry until they were thirty years old, so John spent thirty years in the desert, from when he was a baby until he began his ministry. But those thirty years were critical to his spiritual development. His time in the desert made him "strong in spirit." The Greek word translated "became strong" is *krataioō*. It means to increase in strength or to empower.[8]

Walking in the spirit and power of Elijah is not an easy task. You will face opposition, both natural and spiritual. You need to be empowered by the Holy Spirit in preparation for the times of opposition, the times of trial, the times of struggle. Strength of spirit is vital for Elijahs. The prophet Elijah had to face Ahab, Jezebel, and hundreds of false prophets. John the Baptist had to face Herod, Herodias, and hundreds of Pharisees and Sadducees. And when you are walking in the spirit and power of Elijah, you too will have to face people in authority and religious leaders who don't know the Lord.

Time in the wilderness also teaches you about simplicity and what things are really important. John the Baptist "was clothed in camel's hair, with a leather belt around his waist; and his food was locusts and wild honey" (Matt. 3:4). John's clothes were simple, and they were actually reminiscent of Elijah's clothes: "They answered him, 'He wore a garment of hair, with a belt of leather about his waist.' And he said, 'It is Elijah the Tishbite'" (2 Kings 1:8, ESV). John's food was very simple as well. Yet even though he didn't wear fancy clothes or eat fancy food, he still fulfilled his assignment. He was still able to prepare the way for the Lord. People still flocked to the wilderness in droves to hear him preach.

John the Baptist wasn't trying to sugarcoat his message. He wasn't trying to be politically correct. He wasn't being tolerant. He wasn't trying to be relevant. He preached it straight: "Repent, for the kingdom of heaven is at hand" (Matt. 3:2). And even though his message was both bold and blunt, Matthew 3:5–6 says, "Then Jerusalem, all Judea, and all the region around the Jordan went out to him and were baptized by him in the Jordan, confessing their sins."

People from an entire province went out into the wilderness to hear John the Baptist preach. They couldn't just jump in their cars and drive either. The overwhelming majority of them would have had to walk for miles to get to where John was preaching. But they still went. And the Bible is clear that they didn't go because John was wearing fancy clothes: "But what did you go out to see? A man clothed in soft garments? Indeed, those who wear soft clothing are in kings' houses. But what did you go out to see? A prophet? Yes, I say to you, and more than a prophet" (Matt. 11:8–9). The people went to the wilderness because they recognized that John was a prophet and that he spoke the truth. The other things didn't matter. That is why Elijahs need to learn about simplicity in the wilderness. The exterior stuff—good, bad, or in between—doesn't matter. It's the truth that matters.

The wilderness is also where you get your voice. You have to go to the wilderness to get your voice. You need the one-on-one time with the Lord. You need Him to prepare you, change you, transform you, cut away the junk that weighs you down and holds you back. Just as water is critically important when you are physically in the desert or wilderness, the living water only Jesus can provide is critically important during a spiritual wilderness time. You need to be washed by the water of the

Word, sanctified and cleansed, and set apart in holiness for your assignment.

Embrace the wilderness as a sacred place where God cultivates your voice and prepares you to be a messenger of His truth. Embrace the unique calling He has placed upon your life and step forward with confidence, knowing that He has equipped you with a voice that will make a lasting impact.

The wilderness is also where you learn to hear from the Lord. It is where you learn to discern His message, the word He has for you, or the word He has for you to preach. Those with the spirit and power of Elijah must learn to hear what the Lord is saying rather than rely on their own wisdom or their own knowledge. The prophecy about John the Baptist in Isaiah 40 says, "The voice said, 'Cry out!'" But the immediate response was not for him to cry out whatever he wanted or whatever he thought should be said. His response was, "What shall I cry?" (v. 6).

When the Lord tells you to speak, you need to make sure you are speaking what He wants you to say. And in order to do that, you need to know how to listen for His voice, for the words the Holy Spirit is giving you. That is why you need wilderness time. You need the opportunity to learn to hear His voice clearly and to distinguish His voice from all the others clamoring for your attention. When you are hidden away in the wilderness with the Lord, it gets rid of background noise so you can more easily tune in to the voice of the Lord and become familiar with it so you know when He is speaking.

Your wilderness time with the Lord is necessary for you to become a voice of one crying in the wilderness:

> The voice of one crying in the wilderness: "Prepare the way of the LORD; make straight in the desert a highway for our God. Every valley shall be exalted and every mountain and hill brought low; the crooked places shall

be made straight and the rough places smooth; the glory of the LORD shall be revealed, and all flesh shall see it together; for the mouth of the LORD has spoken."

—ISAIAH 40:3–5

THE CUTTING EDGE

One of the reasons strength of spirit is so important for the Elijah calling is that you are going to be on the cutting edge. As a prophet you will be what your generation needs—but they will despise you. Like John the Baptist, you'll be cutting edge, all right.

When applied to the spirit and power of Elijah, the term *cutting edge* suggests that Elijah operated in a way that was ahead of his time and that he stood out as a pioneer in his prophetic ministry. He was at the forefront of confronting spiritual and moral issues of his era, challenging the prevailing norms and ideologies. Elijah's ministry demonstrated boldness, courage, and a willingness to take risks in obedience to God's calling. He confronted idolatry, false prophets, and the wickedness of his time, fearlessly proclaiming God's truth and demonstrating His power through miraculous signs and wonders.

The spirit and power of Elijah embody a pioneering and transformative approach to ministry. This calling stands out as an example of being on the cutting edge of prophetic insight, discernment, and action. It challenges the status quo, disrupts complacency, and calls for radical change.

Just as Elijah's ministry was marked by a cutting-edge prophetic anointing, prophets today can seek to operate in the same spirit. By being sensitive to the Holy Spirit, embracing boldness and innovation, and staying grounded in God's Word, they can have a cutting-edge impact on their generation, confronting the spiritual challenges and cultural issues of the present age.

Elijahs do not pull their punches. Elijahs are called to turn the hearts of people back to the Lord, and you can't turn back to the Lord unless you repent. Preaching repentance makes you very unpopular with people who do not want to repent or think they have no need to repent. People who have redefined the truth to excuse their actions do not like being called to repent.

That is what happened with Jezebel; when she found out Elijah had executed all her false prophets, she wanted him dead. She sent a messenger to him, saying, "So let the gods do to me, and more also, if I do not make your life as the life of one of them by tomorrow about this time" (1 Kings 19:2).

That is also what happened with John the Baptist. He rebuked Herod for many things, including marrying Herodias, his brother's wife. Herodias had to divorce Herod's brother Philip in order to marry Herod, and that was a clear violation of the Law. Herodias was not happy about the rebuke because it pointed out her sin as well. She wanted John the Baptist's head on a platter, and that is exactly what she got. Even though Herod ordered John to be arrested and thrown into prison, he was afraid to kill him since the people knew John was a prophet. But Herodias connived and plotted, and when the opportunity arose, she forced Herod's hand. John the Baptist was beheaded, and his head was brought on a platter to Herodias' daughter, who in turn gave the head to her mother.

When you are walking in the spirit and power of Elijah, your neck may be right up against the cutting edge of a sword, so to speak. The word of righteousness and repentance from idols like money, power, and control will not keep you in the favor of those who benefit from those idols. The powerful and influential ones will be ready to cut off your head, just as they did with John the Baptist. But you still need to speak the truth. You still need to fulfill your assignment. That is why being rooted and grounded in the Word is important. That is why being able to recognize the voice of the Lord is important. That is why being filled with His righteousness is important.

That is why being strong in spirit is important. That is why you need to have time hidden with the Lord in the wilderness.

Both Elijah and John the Baptist faced significant opposition, threats to their lives, and persecution for their prophetic ministries. However, their steadfastness, faithfulness to God's call, and unwavering commitment to the truth left an indelible impact on history and continue to inspire believers today. It is important to recognize and anticipate these potential challenges and develop resilience and perseverance to navigate the backlash. Staying rooted in your convictions, seeking wise counsel, and embracing a growth mindset can help you overcome obstacles and continue making meaningful progress on the cutting edge.

Chapter 4

Unction

*E*LIJAH HAD A unique quality: he moved by the unction of the Holy Spirit. This unction empowered him to step into the spirit and pull out a prophetic mandate for a nation. Unction is a driver for Elijah prophets, and they need to build it and stir it up as they carry out the mandates of God.

WHAT IS UNCTION?

The word *unction* is not a word we hear very often. *Merriam-Webster* defines *unction* as "the act of anointing as a rite of consecration or healing...spiritual fervor or the expression of such fervor."[1] *Unction* appears only once in the King James Version of the Bible:

> But ye have an unction from the Holy One, and ye know all things.
>
> —1 JOHN 2:20, KJV

The Greek word translated "unction" is *chrisma*. It means an unguent or ointment, a smearing. It also means anointing.[2] In fact, many Bible translations use the word *anointing* instead of *unction*. *Chrisma* is used in one other verse in the New Testament:

> But the *anointing* which you have received from Him abides in you, and you do not need that anyone teach you; but as the same *anointing* teaches you concerning all things, and is true, and is not a lie, and just as it has taught you, you will abide in Him.
> —1 JOHN 2:27, EMPHASIS ADDED

Chrisma comes from the Greek word *chriō*, which means to smear or rub with oil, to consecrate, to anoint.[3] It is used in the Greek translation of the Isaiah 61 prophecy that Jesus read aloud in the synagogue in Nazareth, which He then declared had been fulfilled:

> The Spirit of the LORD is upon Me, because He has anointed Me to preach the gospel to the poor; He has sent Me to heal the brokenhearted, to proclaim liberty to the captives and recovery of sight to the blind, to set at liberty those who are oppressed; to proclaim the acceptable year of the LORD.
> —LUKE 4:18–19

The word is also used in verses such as 2 Corinthians 1:21: "Now He who establishes us with you in Christ and has anointed us is God."

The comparable Hebrew word for *unction* or *anointing* is *māšhâ*. It refers to the holy oil used to anoint Aaron and the other priests for service in the tabernacle or temple of the Lord.[4] It comes from the root word *māšah*, which means to rub with oil or anoint.[5] And both *chriō* and *mašaḥ* are the root words of the word *Messiah*, which means anointed one.

Unction is the anointing of the Holy Spirit. When the Holy Spirit abides in us, if we are in tune with His voice, He will teach us, direct us, guide us, give us words to speak, show us things to do. He causes us to walk in truth. His will be the voice when "your ears shall hear a word behind you, saying, 'This is the way, walk in it,' whenever you turn to the right hand or whenever you turn to the left" (Isa. 30:21).

IN THE DRIVER'S SEAT

Unction is the direction of the Holy Spirit. It will drive you to something or away from something. It will direct your paths. But to be led by the Holy Spirit and experience His unction at work in your life, you need to have a personal relationship with the Holy Spirit.

That personal relationship fosters trust in the Lord. If you don't have that trust, when the time comes to step out in faith and do something that seems crazy or defies what your logical mind is telling you to do, you will hesitate, question, delay, or even fail to carry out your assignment. Proverbs 3:5–6 says, "Trust in the LORD with all your heart, and lean not on your own understanding; in all your ways acknowledge Him, and He shall direct your paths." Elijah prophets need to have the Holy Spirit in the driver's seat, which is why trust is critical for them. It is hard to trust someone you don't know. That is why your time in the wilderness is so vital. You must develop an intimate relationship with the Holy Ghost.

A close relationship with the Holy Spirit also develops your sensitivity to the Spirit and to things happening in the spiritual world. This is also vital for those walking in the spirit and power of Elijah. As prophets called to preach repentance and call people to turn their hearts back to the Lord, it is all too easy for Elijah prophets to forget who the battle is really against. Ephesians 6:12 reminds us, "For we do not wrestle against flesh and blood, but against principalities, against powers, against the rulers of the darkness of this age, against spiritual hosts of wickedness in the heavenly places."

When we are coming against the forces of darkness, preaching the truth of the Word of God with clarity and boldness, there is going to be a battle. And many times Satan will use flesh and blood to wage an all-out war against us. But we must remember that our battle is never against flesh and blood. Our battle is against the demonic powers behind the words and actions of flesh and blood. Our battle is against Satan and his spiritual hosts of wickedness. They are the ones we are called to fight against. And we must always remember one vital thing in every skirmish, every battle, every all-out war: "the battle is the LORD's" (1 Sam. 17:47).

Unction is about being led by the Holy One and letting Him steer you in the right direction, accelerating you into the next season at the right time, or hitting the brakes if the situation warrants. It is also about listening to what the Holy Spirit is speaking to you. Jesus said, "When He, the Spirit of truth, has come, He will guide you into all truth; for He will not speak on His own authority, but whatever He hears He will speak; and He will tell you things to come" (John 16:13). The Holy Ghost is the One who will guide us, direct us, and give us words of truth to speak.

In fact, when we get the unction from the Holy Spirit, many times we get the words He wants us to speak right on the spot. But again, for that to happen, you must have a personal relationship with the Holy Spirit. We need the boldness that comes from the Holy Spirit. The words we speak as Elijah prophets are not preconceived. They are not coming from our own personal agendas. They are coming straight from the heart of God.

That is why the experience in the wilderness is so critical. You need that time hidden away with the Lord. You need the time of refreshing, of spiritual growth, of feasting on and being washed by the water of the Word, of learning to hear the Spirit's voice—and developing your own voice. You need to be in that place of cutting away and dying to self to have the unction of the Holy Ghost.

STUMBLING BLOCKS

There are things that can get in the way of the unction of the Holy Spirit and hinder us from fulfilling our assignments. I call these stumbling blocks to the prophetic. As I said in *The Prophetic Advantage*:

> Accuracy is important to the prophet's ministry. Accuracy is defined as the quality or state of being correct or precise. There are things that can hinder and block accuracy, such as prejudices, misconceptions, doctrinal obsessions, sectarian views, bitterness, rejection, and lust.[6]

We talked about prejudices in the last chapter, and if you are struggling in that area you definitely need to repent. But there are other stumbling blocks too. Mixing up your own opinions and views with the truth of what the Lord is saying is a big one for Elijah prophets. Remember, God's thoughts are higher than your thoughts, and His ways are higher than your ways (Isa. 55:8–9). Never become narrow-minded or dogmatic about the revelations the Lord is giving you. If God starts speaking something new to you, be open to it. Stay tuned in to His voice, not the thoughts and inclinations of your own heart and mind.

Fear of man is another potential stumbling block to walking in the spirit and power of Elijah. Elijah could have chosen to give in to fear of Ahab and Jezebel. John the Baptist could have chosen to give in to fear of Herod and Herodias or fear of the Pharisees. And the Elijah prophets of today could choose to give in to the fear of whomever the enemy sends against them. But the Word of God says that "the fear of man brings a snare" (Prov. 29:25). Fear of man is a trap, so don't fall for it. The fear of the Lord, on the other hand, is anything but a trap. The Word says:

> The secret of the LORD is with those who fear Him.
> —PSALM 25:14

> He will bless those who fear the LORD, both small and great.
> —PSALM 115:13

> The fear of the LORD is the beginning of wisdom, and the knowledge of the Holy One is understanding.
> —PROVERBS 9:10

> In the fear of the LORD there is strong confidence, and His children will have a place of refuge.
> —PROVERBS 14:26

> The fear of the LORD is a fountain of life, to turn one away from the snares of death.
> —PROVERBS 14:27

> The fear of the LORD leads to life, and he who has it will abide in satisfaction.
> —PROVERBS 19:23

We overcome fear of man with the fear of the Lord. We overcome fear of man with faith. We overcome fear of man with love, for "perfect love casts out fear" (1 John 4:18).

Another common stumbling block is being a respecter of persons. When the apostle Peter was preaching to Cornelius' household, he said, "In truth I perceive that God shows no partiality" (Acts 10:34). Other translations say that "God is no respecter of persons" (MEV). Respect of persons is often a religious spirit, causing people to try to limit their ministry to a certain denomination. Respect of persons can also be rooted in prejudice. But regardless of its source, it is a stumbling block for Elijah prophets. James 2:9 says, "But if you show partiality, you commit sin, and are convicted by the law as transgressors." To walk in the spirit and power of Elijah, you must deliver the heart of God without partiality.

Human compassion—having compassion for something God is judging—is another potential stumbling block for Elijah prophets. You cannot allow human compassion to affect your prophetic flow. Ministering correction to people you love is difficult, but you are called to obey the Spirit. You are called to walk in the Spirit. When the Holy Spirit is prompting you to speak, failing to speak out of misplaced compassion is actually unloving. Prophesying truth brings deliverance to the hearer. Don't leave someone you care about chained up in bondage to sin out of what you think is compassion. Jesus wants them to walk in freedom. Proclaim liberty to the captives.

Your time in the wilderness with the Lord will help with overcoming whatever stumbling blocks you are facing. To come against the stumbling blocks, you must first desire truth in your inward parts:

> Behold, You desire truth in the inward parts, and in the hidden part You will make me to know wisdom.
> —PSALM 51:6

You need to desire the real truth, the truth of the Lord that reaches down all the way into the depth of your being. Don't be led astray by any kind of deception, especially self-deception. It takes the mercy and power of the Holy Spirit to break through deception.

Next, allow the Holy Spirit to search your heart:

> Search me, O God, and know my heart; try me, and know my anxieties; and see if there is any wicked way in me, and lead me in the way everlasting.
>
> —PSALM 139:23–24

The Holy Spirit is the Spirit of truth. He will give you the wisdom you need to root out any issues in your heart that may cause you to stumble. When the Holy Spirit reveals the flaws and failings in your heart, be humble and honest with yourself rather than trying to justify your actions and attitudes. Humility and honesty are needed for healing and deliverance to occur.

The next step is to repent immediately. Delaying your response to what the Holy Spirit has shown you will only hurt you since the delay can lead to hardness of heart and even to more deception. And remember that delayed obedience is disobedience.

> Come, and let us return to the LORD; for He has torn, but He will heal us; He has stricken, but He will bind us up.
>
> —HOSEA 6:1

> As many as I love, I rebuke and chasten. Therefore be zealous and repent.
>
> —REVELATION 3:19

The last step is to rend your heart. Rending one's garments is a sign of grief or desperation that was practiced often in the Bible and is still practiced by some Jewish people today. However,

God doesn't want a grief that is only on the surface. He wants to see a change in your heart. That is why the Word says:

> "Now, therefore," says the LORD, "Turn to Me with all your heart, with fasting, with weeping, and with mourning." So rend your heart, and not your garments; return to the LORD your God, for He is gracious and merciful, slow to anger, and of great kindness.
> —JOEL 2:12–13

You need to tear your heart away from anything and everything in your life that will be a stumbling block to walking in the spirit and power of Elijah, anything and everything that will block the flow of the Holy Ghost. If you are stuck in patterns of sin, some tearing will be required for you to be set free. But Jesus wants you living and walking in freedom. Don't stay bound up in the shackles of your sin. Deal radically with your issues—all your hang-ups and hiccups and hardness of heart—and be delivered and set free!

STIR IT UP!

Unction comes from the Holy Spirit. There is no other way to get it. You can't manufacture it. You can't fake it. You can't buy it. You can't get it by pulling yourself up by your bootstraps. You can't get it by doing good deeds. You can't get it by reading about it or hearing about it or talking about it. You can't get it with might or power either.

> "Not by might nor by power, but by My Spirit," says the LORD of hosts.
> —ZECHARIAH 4:6

Unction only comes from being in a close, personal relationship with the Holy Spirit. There is no substitute for it. It starts in your wilderness time, in your waiting time. After God has purified and refined our hearts is when He begins to give us the unction. When you are bound together with the Lord, He will become your source—for everything. And that closeness, that solid relationship, that connection with the Holy Ghost is the firm foundation you need to walk in the spirit and power of Elijah.

I also believe the Lord gives you unction for specific things that no one else can preach but you. The message becomes your mark of distinction. You are uniquely designed, created, equipped, and called to bring a specific message to this generation, and I believe the Holy Spirit will give you the unction to preach that message. That doesn't mean you don't need to study and meditate on the Word, spend time in prayer, seek the Lord's face, and prepare to preach a message. You need to do all those things, because those are all ways the Holy Spirit speaks to you.

The unction of the Holy Spirit will lead you to specific passages of Scripture. The unction will drive you to search and seek the Lord in prayer until an answer is given. God promised that His Word will never return to Him void but will accomplish what He sent it forth to do (Isa. 55:11), so time in the Word is never a waste. Nor is spending time with the Lord ever a waste. The more time you spend with Him, the more easily you will recognize His voice, recognize His direction, recognize His unction. You need to do the work in the natural to study and read about the message God is laying on your heart, but you also need to recognize that unction comes from the Holy Spirit, not from any of your preconceived notions. So do your part, but then be open to whatever, whoever, and wherever the Spirit leads.

Praying in the Holy Spirit is another way to build yourself up: "But you, beloved, building yourselves up on your most holy faith, praying in the Holy Spirit, keep yourselves in the love of God, looking for the mercy of our Lord Jesus Christ unto eternal life" (Jude 20–21).

For it is the Lord who stirs up your spirit and impresses that unction on you. There are multiple examples of the Lord stirring up someone's spirit in the Bible:

> So the God of Israel stirred up the spirit of Pul king of Assyria, that is, Tiglath-Pileser king of Assyria. He carried the Reubenites, the Gadites, and the half-tribe of Manasseh into captivity.
>
> —1 Chronicles 5:26

> Now in the first year of Cyrus king of Persia, that the word of the Lord by the mouth of Jeremiah might be fulfilled, the Lord stirred up the spirit of Cyrus king of Persia, so that he made a proclamation throughout all his kingdom, and also put it in writing, saying,
>
> Thus says Cyrus king of Persia:
>
> All the kingdoms of the earth the Lord God of heaven has given me. And He has commanded me to build Him a house at Jerusalem which is in Judah. Who is among you of all His people? May the Lord his God be with him, and let him go up!
>
> —2 Chronicles 36:22–23

> Then Zerubbabel the son of Shealtiel, and Joshua the son of Jehozadak, the high priest, with all the remnant of the people, obeyed the voice of the Lord their God, and the words of Haggai the prophet, as the Lord their God had sent him; and the people feared the presence of the Lord. Then Haggai, the Lord's messenger, spoke the Lord's message to the people, saying, "I am with you, says the Lord." So the Lord stirred up the spirit of Zerubbabel the son of Shealtiel, governor of Judah, and the spirit of Joshua the son of Jehozadak, the high priest, and the spirit of all the remnant of the people; and they came and worked on the house of the Lord of hosts, their God.
>
> —Haggai 1:12–14

I want you to notice some things about these examples. In the first example, God stirred up someone's spirit to execute judgment. As an Elijah, there may be times when God is calling you to be a voice of judgment, not out of hatred or your own sense of who should or should not be judged, but rather out of the love of God for a people who have turned away from Him. "The judgments of the LORD are true and righteous altogether" (Ps. 19:9). The judgments of the Lord are there to help, not to harm: "Let Your judgments help me" (Ps. 119:175). They help us learn and grow: "For when Your judgments are in the earth, the inhabitants of the world will learn righteousness" (Isa. 26:9).

If God gives you the unction to speak words of judgment, it is so that the people might repent, turn from their wicked ways, and be restored to right relationship with Him. It is an act of love, calling the prodigals to return to the Father who loves them. This demonstrates God's involvement in human affairs and His ability to awaken and inspire individuals for a specific purpose.

The second example shows us that God stirred up the spirit of someone who recognized who his source was. Cyrus was the king of a great empire, but he knew who placed him in that position and kept him there. He knew that the Lord was the One who had given him all that he had. He was a mighty king, but he humbly recognized the truth. Those who walk in the spirit and power of Elijah need to do the same.

The Lord is the one who made you a prophet. He gave you a good and marvelous gift. He is the source of that gift, the source of all that you have—all your blessings, all your wisdom, all your power, all your peace, all your joy, all your everything. Don't make the mistake of letting pride get in the way. Don't fall into the trap of thinking you earned your gifts or that you are better than others because of your gifts. Everything you have comes from the Lord, and He alone deserves the glory. So walk in humility, no matter what position you are elevated to while still on this earth.

> He has shown you, O man, what is good; and what does
> the LORD require of you but to do justly, to love mercy,
> and to walk humbly with your God?
>
> —MICAH 6:8

The third example is one of the Lord stirring up the spirits of an entire group of people. But notice what happened first: "Then Zerubbabel...and Joshua...with all the remnant of the people, *obeyed* the voice of the Lord their God" (Hag. 1:12, emphasis added). They obeyed. Don't miss that. If you want the unction of the Holy Spirit—if you want Him to stir you to act or speak—start by obeying. Obedience leads to righteousness (Rom. 6:16).

> For You, O LORD, will bless the righteous; with favor
> You will surround him as with a shield.
>
> —PSALM 5:12

You cannot be a voice calling for people to repent and turn from their unrighteousness if you are walking in unrighteousness yourself. You need to have clean hands and a pure heart. And whenever you are in a place where you are stuck in sin again, or you discover darkness hiding in your heart, or you realize your hands are anything but clean, get to the wilderness again. Hide yourself away with the Lord so He can purify you and refine you once again. Then offer Him the sacrifice of obedience. Show Him you love Him by your willingness to obey His Word and walk in His ways.

The Holy Spirit is the One who gives you the unction and also the One who stirs it up. He will stir up your passion, your zeal. You just need to do your part to be ready.

Chapter 5

Word and Deed

*E*LIJAH WAS A prophet of both word and deed. Being a prophet is about more than what you say; it is also about what you do. As an Elijah prophet, your words and actions should work together to grow the kingdom of God, bring hope and healing, turn hearts back to the heavenly Father, demonstrate righteousness, and preach the truth.

Elijah's prophetic mantle was not one of mere rhetoric. No, it was one of action, of stepping boldly into the supernatural and partnering with the divine in extraordinary ways. He walked in the power of God as a conduit through which miracles were birthed and transformation unfolded. From the moment he spoke to the heavens, commanding rain to fall upon parched earth, to the day he raised the widow's son from the grip of death, his deeds were marked with undeniable authority.

In this hour, as we stand at the crossroads of destiny, the prophetic call resonates within our own hearts. We are called to be a generation that speaks with boldness, uttering words that shift atmospheres and shake the foundations of darkness. Our tongues, ignited by the fire of the Holy Spirit, must declare the heart of God, releasing divine decrees that bring forth His purposes upon the earth.

WORD POWER

As a prophet, your words are important. Your words have power. Prophets are called to be the mouthpiece of the Lord in the earth.

Elijah spoke words of power over and over again throughout his ministry. In fact, the very first mention of Elijah in the Bible is when he said, "As the LORD God of Israel lives, before whom I stand, there shall not be dew nor rain these years, except at my word" (1 Kings 17:1). Elijah, with the unction of the Lord, spoke a word that brought about a drought in the land of Israel. And the very words he spoke declared that he knew it was his words that would put a stop to the drought when the time was right.

As a prophet, you cannot underestimate the power of your words. God spoke the world and everything in it into existence with the spoken Word. The Bible says, "Death and life are in the power of the tongue" (Prov. 18:21). The words you speak as a prophet in the spirit and power of Elijah will either bring life or death, so you must choose your words wisely. When you speak as prophet, you must speak with the unction of the Holy Spirit, and you must speak the words He is giving you—not the words of your own heart or mind.

In the Bible, God was always very clear with the prophets. When Jeremiah was afraid to speak as a prophet, the Lord told him,

> "For you shall go to all to whom I send you, and whatever I command you, you shall speak. Do not be afraid

of their faces, for I am with you to deliver you," says
the LORD.

Then the LORD put forth His hand and touched my
mouth, and the LORD said to me: "Behold, I have put
My words in your mouth. See, I have this day set you
over the nations and over the kingdoms, to root out and
to pull down, to destroy and to throw down, to build
and to plant."

—JEREMIAH 1:7–10

The same thing happens with the words of Elijah prophets. When they are speaking the words of the Lord, their
words have the power to root out and pull down strongholds
of idolatry, unrighteousness, bitterness, greed, envy, and lust.
Their words have the power to destroy and pull down the lies
and schemes of the enemy and the works of darkness coming
against the children of God. Their words have the power to
build and to plant hope, peace, repentance, forgiveness, mercy,
grace, love, and joy in the hearts of believers as they turn back
to the Lord, to follow Him in all His ways.

The words of prophets can pierce right to the heart of a
matter. When the people gathered on Mount Carmel for the
face-off between Elijah and the prophets of Baal, Elijah asked
that key question: "How long will you falter between two
opinions? If the LORD is God, follow Him; but if Baal, follow
him" (1 Kings 18:21). But his words didn't stop there. And at
the time of the evening sacrifice, he declared the truth with
boldness and unreserved power. He spoke the words the Lord
had given him, and those words also spoke right to the heart
of the matter: the hearts of the children of Israel.

LORD God of Abraham, Isaac, and Israel, let it be known
this day that You are God in Israel and I am Your servant, and that I have done all these things at Your word.
Hear me, O LORD, hear me, that this people may know

that You are the LORD God, and that You have turned
their hearts back to You again.

—1 KINGS 18:36–37

Everything Elijah said and did was at God's word. He
acknowledged his position as a servant of the Lord, and he
obeyed the way a humble servant does. And when you obey
and declare the truth just the way God told you to, the Lord
is going to show up:

Then the fire of the LORD fell and consumed the burnt
sacrifice, and the wood and the stones and the dust, and
it licked up the water that was in the trench.

—1 KINGS 18:38

God responded to the words of Elijah. He responds to your
words too. Never forget the power you possess in your words.

Another thing you must always remember as a prophet is
the Lord's command to Ezekiel: "You shall speak My words to
them, whether they hear or whether they refuse" (Ezek. 2:7).
As a prophet, you must speak when the Holy Spirit gives you
the unction to speak. You are responsible to obey, but you are
not responsible for making others listen or respond to the word
you have spoken. That is on them. It is not your job to inter-
pret the message. Watch for fulfillment of the message. You
just need to be faithful to say and do whatever the Lord says to
say and do, and then let the Holy Spirit working in the hearts
of people do the rest.

ADVANTAGES OF THE WORD OF THE LORD

The word of the Lord brings great benefits to believers. There is
a list of one hundred advantages of the word of the Lord in my
book *The Prophetic Advantage*.[1] Here are just a few examples:

The word of the Lord brings healing and deliverance.

He sent His word and healed them, and delivered them
from their destructions.

—PSALM 107:20

The prophetic word shines a light into dark places.

And so we have the prophetic word confirmed, which
you do well to heed as a light that shines in a dark
place, until the day dawns and the morning star rises
in your hearts.

—2 PETER 1:19

The word of the Lord is a fire that can burn away the dead,
dry things in your life. It is also a hammer that breaks even
the hardest of hearts so it can be made whole and clean again.

"Is not My word like a fire?" says the LORD, "And like a
hammer that breaks the rock in pieces?"

—JEREMIAH 23:29

The word of the Lord refreshes like rain, bringing life and
new growth.

Let my teaching drop as the rain, my speech distill as
the dew, as raindrops on the tender herb, and as showers
on the grass.

—DEUTERONOMY 32:2

The prophetic word imparts vision and purpose to the children of God.

Where there is no vision, the people perish; but happy is
he who keeps the teaching.

—PROVERBS 29:18, MEV

The Lord reveals Himself through the prophetic word.

> Then the LORD appeared again in Shiloh. For the LORD revealed Himself to Samuel in Shiloh by the word of the LORD.
>
> —1 SAMUEL 3:21

The word of the Lord destroys the spirit of Jezebel.

> Therefore they came back and told him. And he said, "This is the word of the LORD, which He spoke by His servant Elijah the Tishbite, saying, 'On the plot of ground at Jezreel dogs shall eat the flesh of Jezebel; and the corpse of Jezebel shall be as refuse on the surface of the field, in the plot at Jezreel, so that they shall not say, "Here lies Jezebel."'"
>
> —2 KINGS 9:36–37

The word of the Lord brings restoration.

> He restored the territory of Israel from the entrance of Hamath to the Sea of the Arabah, according to the word of the Lord God of Israel, which He had spoken through His servant Jonah the son of Amittai, the prophet who was from Gath Hepher.
>
> —2 KINGS 14:25

The word of the Lord gives hope.

> I wait for the LORD, my soul waits, and in His word I do hope.
>
> —PSALM 130:5

The prophetic word gives you courage to do acts of righteousness, even when they go against the culture's standards.

> And when Asa heard these words and the prophecy of Oded the prophet, he took courage, and removed the abominable idols from all the land of Judah and

Benjamin and from the cities which he had taken in the mountains of Ephraim; and he restored the altar of the LORD that was before the vestibule of the LORD.

—2 CHRONICLES 15:8

FAITH WORKS

While speaking, preaching, and declaring the word of the Lord is a major part of walking in the spirit and power of Elijah, it is not the only part. Elijah was also a man of action. He was a prophet who did the works of the Lord.

"Actions speak louder than words" is a saying we hear often, and it is very true. There are many layers to this concept for Elijah prophets. This first has to do with personal behavior and righteousness. To walk in the spirit and power of Elijah, you must walk in righteousness. You must have clean hands and a pure heart. If you are struggling with habitual sin, you need to repent. Get into the wilderness with the Lord, and allow Him to cleanse you and refine you with His Word. Seek first the Lord and His righteousness. This is vital because sin can nullify your ministry before it even starts. You can't expect someone to heed the word of the Lord you speak if they know you are having an affair or they see you falling-down drunk at the bar every Friday night. You also can't expect to hear clearly from the Lord if your heart is hardened by sin or your ears are stopped up by the lies you are telling yourself to justify your sin.

Beyond your personal actions, your actions toward others also speak much louder than your words. As a man or woman of God, your actions should point to Jesus. They should be a reflection of the heart of the Lord for His people.

He has shown you, O man, what is good; and what does the LORD require of you but to do justly, to love mercy, and to walk humbly with your God?

—MICAH 6:8

By this all will know that you are My disciples, if you have love for one another.

—John 13:35

Walk worthy of the calling with which you were called, with all lowliness and gentleness, with longsuffering, bearing with one another in love, endeavoring to keep the unity of the Spirit in the bond of peace.

—Ephesians 4:1–3

Therefore, whatever you want men to do to you, do also to them, for this is the Law and the Prophets.

—Matthew 7:12

Let each of you look out not only for his own interests, but also for the interests of others.

—Philippians 2:4

The Book of James clearly states that faith without works is dead:

> If a brother or sister is naked and destitute of daily food, and one of you says to them, "Depart in peace, be warmed and filled," but you do not give them the things which are needed for the body, what does it profit? Thus also faith by itself, if it does not have works, is dead. But someone will say, "You have faith, and I have works." Show me your faith without your works, and I will show you my faith by my works.... For as the body without the spirit is dead, so faith without works is dead also.
>
> —James 2:15–18, 26

Faith works. Faith does something. While faith prays and speaks and preaches, it also puts actions behind the words. Elijah didn't just preach against idolatry—he did something about it. He didn't just say the Lord was greater than any false god or idol—he showed it. And when the Lord told him to go, he went. When the Lord told him to run, he ran.

As children of God walking in the spirit and power of Elijah, we need to pray and then act. We need to seek the Lord for His direction, for His word, and then act upon what He tells us to do. God has called us to show His love to a world desperately in need of it. God has called us to love one another. God has called us to put His love into action. Love is an action word.

MOVED WITH COMPASSION

When Jesus walked the earth, He was a man of the Word. He spoke the Word, shared the wisdom of the Lord, preached righteousness, declared the truth, and spoke words of hope, healing, faith, peace, and compassion. But Jesus didn't just speak; He acted.

The Bible says over and over again that Jesus was moved with compassion for people:

> But when He saw the multitudes, He was moved with compassion for them, because they were weary and scattered, like sheep having no shepherd.
> —MATTHEW 9:36

> And when Jesus went out He saw a great multitude; and He was moved with compassion for them, and healed their sick.
> —MATTHEW 14:14

> Now Jesus called His disciples to Himself and said, "I have compassion on the multitude, because they have now continued with Me three days and have nothing to eat. And I do not want to send them away hungry, lest they faint on the way."
> —MATTHEW 15:32

> And Jesus, when He came out, saw a great multitude
> and was moved with compassion for them, because they
> were like sheep not having a shepherd. So He began to
> teach them many things.
>
> —MARK 6:34

Jesus had compassion for people lacking direction and hope. He had compassion for people lacking someone to guide them and help them and see to their needs. He had compassion for the weary—both of body and spirit. He had compassion for the sick, the injured, and the wounded. He had compassion for the hungry and the poor. Part of Jesus' assignment on the earth was this:

> The Spirit of the LORD God is upon Me, because the
> LORD has anointed Me to preach good tidings to the
> poor; He has sent Me to heal the brokenhearted, to pro-
> claim liberty to the captives, and the opening of the
> prison to those who are bound; to proclaim the accept-
> able year of the LORD, and the day of vengeance of our
> God; to comfort all who mourn, to console those who
> mourn in Zion, to give them beauty for ashes, the oil of
> joy for mourning, the garment of praise for the spirit of
> heaviness; that they may be called trees of righteousness,
> the planting of the LORD, that He may be glorified.
>
> —ISAIAH 61:1–3

Jesus fulfilled His assignment. He touched lepers and healed them. He made the blind see, the lame walk, and the deaf hear. He healed the wounded heart of the woman caught in adultery by not condemning and instead telling her to go and sin no more. He overturned the tables of the moneychangers who made the house of the Lord a den of thieves. He fed the hungry. He quenched the thirst of many—both physically and spiritually. He freed people in bondage to demons. He set at liberty those chained up by their sin. He lifted people from the ashes of their brokenness and gave them a crown of beauty. He redeemed and restored. He demonstrated the power of God with miracles, signs, and wonders.

Jesus showed us that love acts.

And He also said, "Most assuredly, I say to you, he who believes in Me, the works that I do he will do also; and greater works than these he will do, because I go to My Father" (John 14:12). You have the ability to do greater works by faith than Jesus did—Jesus Himself said so. Operating in the prophetic isn't just about lip service. It is about God's love and compassion in action. Miracles, signs, and wonders are extensions of God's love to us. When you are operating in the spirit and power of Elijah and your heart is moved with compassion, you can do miracles, signs, and wonders at the unction of the Holy Spirit. When a prophet heals or helps someone find their way to provision and prosperity, it is an enactment of God's love.

WORD AND DEED WORKING TOGETHER

Your actions as a prophet in the spirit and power of Elijah will also give credibility to your words as you are led by the Holy Spirit and respond to His unction. Early in his ministry, Elijah encountered a widow with a son. The Lord had specifically directed Elijah to go to Zarephath, saying, "I have commanded a widow there to provide for you" (1 Kings 17:9). The widow was not a rich woman—she was quite poor in fact—but she was a woman of faith.

Elijah came across the woman gathering sticks at the gate of the city, and he asked her for some water and a morsel of bread. The woman replied, "As the LORD your God lives, I do not have bread, only a handful of flour in a bin, and a little oil in a jar; and see, I am gathering a couple of sticks that I may go in and prepare it for myself and my son, that we may eat it, and die" (1 Kings 17:12). The woman had reached the end of her rope. She was down to a handful of flour and a little oil, and then that would be the end. She and her son would eat it and then starve to death since she had no way to provide for herself and her son. Because there was a drought, everyone was suffering, and the people who might normally have helped the widow and her son with food were struggling to put food on the table themselves. The poor widow had no hope.

But then Elijah appeared. When she informed him of her situation, he responded, "Do not fear; go and do as you have said, but make me a small cake from it first, and bring it to me; and afterward make some for yourself and your son. For thus says the LORD God of Israel: 'The bin of flour shall not be used up, nor shall the jar of oil run dry, until the day the LORD sends rain on the earth'" (1 Kings 17:13–14).

The woman stepped out in faith, and she did exactly what Elijah said to do. And just as Elijah had said, "The bin of flour was not used up, nor did the jar of oil run dry, according to the word of the LORD which He spoke by Elijah" (1 Kings 17:16).

But then tragedy struck. The widow's son got sick and died. So the widow said to Elijah, "What have I to do with you, O man of God? Have you come to me to bring my sin to remembrance, and to kill my son?" (1 Kings 17:18). The widow knew she wasn't perfect. She knew she had sin in her past. She also knew that Elijah was a man of God, so she assumed that the death of her son was a judgment for her past sins, even though she had responded to Elijah in faith and provided food and shelter for him.

It is like that sometimes when you're a prophet. You see the hand of the Lord at work. He speaks to you, you respond in obedience, and things work out exactly the way the Lord said they would. He works miracles on your behalf and on behalf of those you are ministering to. But then something unexpected happens. Something happens that doesn't seem to make sense, that challenges your faith and makes you wonder if you really heard from the Lord correctly.

When those moments happen, it is all the more important that you stay tuned in to the Holy Spirit, listening for His leading, responding to His unction, and acting in faith and obedience to His word to you. The life of a prophet is never an easy one, so these challenges to your faith will happen. And how you react to the challenges matters. One profound truth I've come to understand is that our Almighty God is never taken aback or caught off guard. He always has a grander plan, one that surpasses our limited human perspective. As the Alpha and Omega, the beginning and the end, He exists outside the constraints of time, knowing every intricate detail of our lives. Nothing that unfolds before us is a surprise to Him. This is a truth Elijah prophets must cultivate in their hearts. God is God, and we are not.

Even in the face of challenging circumstances or unexpected events, we can find solace in the fact that God's wisdom and sovereignty prevail. He orchestrates every situation, weaving a tapestry that ultimately brings glory to His name. In His infinite wisdom, He foresaw the very moments we find ourselves in and has already devised a strategic plan to manifest His purposes.

Elijah responded to the widow by asking her to give him her son.

> So he took him out of her arms and carried him to the upper room where he was staying, and laid him on his own bed. Then he cried out to the LORD and said, "O LORD my God, have You also brought tragedy on the widow with whom I lodge, by killing her son?" And he stretched himself out on the child three times, and cried out to the LORD and said, "O LORD my God, I pray, let this child's soul come back to him." Then the LORD heard the voice of Elijah; and the soul of the child came back to him, and he revived. And Elijah took the

child and brought him down from the upper room into
the house, and gave him to his mother. And Elijah said,
"See, your son lives!"

—1 KINGS 17:19–23

Elijah worked a miracle. He responded in obedience to
the unction of the Lord, and he raised the widow's son from
the dead. When you are in close relationship with the Lord,
walking in righteousness before Him, listening to His voice,
responding to His unction in obedience and faith, you will
walk in miracles, signs, and wonders—all to the glory of God.
Remember, there is nothing too hard for God, and with God
all things are possible (Jer. 32:17; Matt. 19:26).

The widow's response to her son being raised from the dead
is important to note. She said, "Now by this I know that you
are a man of God, and that the word of the LORD in your
mouth is the truth" (1 Kings 17:24). The widow already knew
Elijah was a man of God. The Lord had removed any doubt
about that by the miracle of the never-ending flour and oil.
But Elijah's latest deed of raising her son from the dead accom-
plished something else—it made her realize without a shadow
of doubt that the word of the Lord that Elijah spoke was true.
Your actions as an Elijah prophet speak to the truth of your
words.

Word and deed are meant to work together. As prophets,
we need to be wary of falling into the trap of pride because we
are the ones hearing from the Lord. Prophets today often get
caught up in being super spiritual and exclusive, as being the
ones who have a word from the Lord. They get caught up in
being honored and known for being a prophet when there are
real people who need a touch from God. The word of the Lord
delivers people, but meeting someone's everyday need delivers people too. And for Elijah, more was written about what
he did than what he said. He activated the angelic realm and

supernatural provision on behalf of God's people. He demonstrated the power of the one true God, and by his words *and* his deeds he turned the hearts of the children of Israel back to the Lord.

The time is ripe for action, for stepping into the supernatural realm and partnering with heaven's agenda. Like Elijah, let us embrace the miraculous, expect the impossible, and move in unwavering faith. Through signs and wonders, we shall see the captives set free, the broken made whole, and the lost brought into the embrace of the Father.

In the footsteps of Elijah, we find an invitation to be vessels of righteousness, carriers of the flame that ignites revival. As we stand upon the threshold of destiny, may we take hold of the prophetic mantle with courage and conviction. Let our words resound with heavenly authority, and our deeds manifest the power of the Almighty.

Beloved, heed the call, for Elijah's legacy beckons us to rise. Embrace the prophetic mantle, and let our words and deeds be a symphony of divine love, a resounding echo of heaven's heart. Together we shall shake nations, transform cities, and usher in the glorious kingdom of our God.

PART II

REFORMATION

Chapter 6

Elijah Is Here

WHEN ELIJAHS EMERGE from their Cherith season, their time hidden with the Lord, the showdown begins. The drought Elijah proclaimed lasted for three years. After his season at the Brook Cherith, he stayed with the widow of Zarephath until the time came for him to emerge on the scene. Zarephath wasn't in Israel, so Elijah was well hidden while he stayed there. Because of the length of the drought, God provided miraculously for Elijah both at the brook and in Zarephath.

Elijah knew the importance of waiting on the Lord's timing, which is why he remained hidden so long. As we have discussed, obedience to the Lord is important. Until Elijah prophets are given the unction of the Holy Spirit to move, they need to stay put. You need to trust that God is still preparing you for the challenges to come and wait on His timing—because when you emerge, it will be time for the showdown.

Present Yourself

It had been three years—three years of drought, three years of waiting, three years of growing, three years of developing his relationship with the Lord, three years of wondering when the time to act would be. Then all of a sudden, "the word of the LORD came to Elijah, in the third year, saying, 'Go, present yourself to Ahab, and I will send rain on the earth'" (1 Kings 18:1).

That verse contains timeless principles that resonate with this generation. To "present yourself" to the kings of the land carries a deeper significance beyond its historical context. In this generation, it speaks to a call to step into positions of influence and authority, both in the secular and spiritual realms. It signifies a divine commission to engage with leaders, decision-makers, and influencers within our spheres of influence.

In the context of this verse, Elijah was instructed to present himself before Ahab, the king of Israel, at a time of drought and spiritual depravity. Elijah's presence before the king served as a catalyst for divine intervention and a confrontation of the prevailing idolatry. Likewise, in this generation, we are called to boldly and fearlessly engage with those in authority, carrying the truth of God's Word and His transformative power.

In this generation, presenting ourselves to the kings of the land demands that we embody integrity, wisdom, and the Spirit of God. It requires a commitment to righteousness, justice, and compassion. We must be bold in speaking truth to power, unafraid to address societal issues and engage in conversations that challenge the prevailing norms.

Elijah's season of being hidden away with the Lord had come to an end; he was ready to obey the unction of the Lord, and he did so immediately. The very next verse begins, "So Elijah went to present himself to Ahab" (v. 2). When you are walking in the spirit and power of Elijah and God tells you to go, you go.

Keep in mind that the last thing Elijah had said to Ahab was, "As the Lord God of Israel lives, before whom I stand, there shall not be dew nor rain these years, except at my word" (1 Kings 17:1). And that is exactly what had happened. Ahab was king over the kingdom that had been dealing with drought and famine for three years because of Elijah's prophetic word. It had reached the point where Ahab himself—the king—was out searching the land for grass to keep his livestock alive with a man named Obadiah, who ran the king's household. Ahab wasn't sitting on his throne, eating bonbons, drinking wine, and doing kingly things. He was out in the sun and heat, searching for springs that might have grass nearby to feed his animals. The effects of the drought had reached even to the palace of the king.

Because of that, Elijah knew he wasn't too popular with Ahab. Yet when the Lord told Elijah to go present himself to Ahab, Elijah didn't hesitate. And that is what Elijahs do. They do not give in to the fear of man. They are not respecters of persons. It doesn't matter who the Lord is sending you to, how powerful they are, what they think of you, what they have the power to do to you—none of that matters in the face of the Holy Spirit telling you to go.

As Elijah was going to present himself to Ahab, he ran into Obadiah. The Bible tells us that "Obadiah feared the Lord greatly" (1 Kings 18:3–4). When Obadiah saw Elijah, he knew immediately who he was, and Obadiah fell on his face. He probably had no idea what to expect, especially given that the last time Elijah appeared, it had been the beginning of the drought that had made his job much more difficult for three years.

Elijah said, "Go, tell your master, 'Elijah is here'" (1 Kings 18:11).

Obadiah confirmed that Ahab was not a fan of Elijah's when he responded,

How have I sinned, that you are delivering your servant into the hand of Ahab, to kill me? As the LORD your God lives, there is no nation or kingdom where my master has not sent someone to hunt for you; and when they said, "He is not here," he took an oath from the kingdom or nation that they could not find you. And now you say, "Go, tell your master, 'Elijah is here'"! And it shall come to pass, as soon as I am gone from you, that the Spirit of the LORD will carry you to a place I do not know; so when I go and tell Ahab, and he cannot find you, he will kill me. But I your servant have feared the LORD from my youth. Was it not reported to my lord what I did when Jezebel killed the prophets of the LORD, how I hid one hundred men of the LORD's prophets, fifty to a cave, and fed them with bread and water? And now you say, "Go, tell your master, 'Elijah is here.'" He will kill me!

—1 KINGS 18:9–14

Obadiah was afraid for his life. He knew all the effort Ahab had put into hunting for Elijah, and he was worried that if he delivered the message and Elijah disappeared before Ahab came back, he would be executed by the evil king. However, Elijah assured Obadiah that he would present himself before Ahab that day, just as the Lord had directed.

Elijah's message to Ahab was bold and straightforward. He was letting Ahab know that he had arrived, and it was time for something to happen. He was also letting Ahab know that things were happening according to the Lord's timing. Ahab had been searching for Elijah for years without success. Yet as soon as the Lord gave the order, Ahab didn't have to look anymore. Elijah came to him.

In Hebrew, Elijah's message for Ahab was actually saying three different things. The New King James Version of the Bible italicizes words that are not actually in the Hebrew or

Greek but have been added for clarity. The message Obadiah was to give Ahab reads, "Elijah *is here*" (1 Kings 18:8). That means *is here* is not in the original Hebrew. So the message Obadiah was to deliver was actually only one word: Elijah.

Now, the message of course means that Elijah was there. That is clear from Obadiah's response. But think back to the meaning of Elijah's name. It means "my God is Jehovah." When Obadiah delivered the message to Ahab, he was also declaring the truth that just like Elijah, Obadiah feared and served the Lord. He was saying, "My God is the Lord." Elijah's name also means "Jehovah is God." So when Obadiah delivered the message, he was declaring the truth that changes everything, the truth that controls the universe, the truth by which nations and kings rise and fall, the truth that carries more power than anything else: "The Lord is God!"

The proclamation "Elijah is here" carries profound implications for present-day prophets and those called to operate in the prophetic giftings. Elijah, as a renowned prophet of old, represents the powerful anointing and mantle of prophetic ministry. His presence symbolizes the manifestation of God's prophetic voice and power in a generation.

To this generation of prophets, the declaration "Elijah is here" signifies the awakening of a divine mandate and anointing. It serves as a reminder that the spirit and essence of Elijah, as a forerunner and catalyst for transformation, dwells within those who are called to prophetic ministry today. God is releasing new mantles of authority, the anointing to bring forth God's messages, and the power to confront and challenge the prevailing spiritual climate.

In this generation, "Elijah is here" calls prophets to embrace their identity and calling as voices of truth and transformation. It is an invitation to operate in the same boldness, courage, and unwavering faith that characterized Elijah's ministry. It implies a mandate to speak uncompromisingly, fearlessly addressing the prevalent idolatry, spiritual apathy, and moral decay of our times. It is time for prophets of today to recognize the weight and importance of their calling. You have been anointed with a mantle of prophetic authority, carrying within you the very essence of Elijah's spirit. Just as Elijah confronted the prevailing spiritual climate of his day, so too are you called to confront the darkness and bring forth the light of God's truth.

Moreover, the declaration "Elijah is here" reminds prophets of their role as agents of revival and restoration. Just as Elijah confronted the prophets of Baal and witnessed the manifestation of God's power, this generation of prophets is called to dismantle the strongholds of darkness and release the transformative power of God's Spirit. The declaration "Elijah is here" signifies a divine commission to bring healing, deliverance, and revival to individuals, communities, and nations.

Furthermore, "Elijah is here" highlights the importance of unity and collaboration among prophets. Just as Elijah was not alone in his prophetic journey but had fellow prophets like Elisha, this generation is called to foster a sense of community, support, and accountability among prophetic voices. Together they can strengthen one another, share insights and revelations, and collectively usher in a powerful move of God.

Ultimately, the declaration "Elijah is here" serves as a clarion call for this generation of prophets to rise up, embracing their divine calling and walking in the authority and anointing of the prophetic mantle. It is an invitation to carry the fire of God's presence, confront the darkness, and release prophetic utterances that bring transformation, revival, and the manifestation of God's kingdom on earth.

TROUBLER OF ISRAEL

When Ahab arrived, he said to Elijah, "Is that you, O troubler of Israel?" (1 Kings 18:17). The Hebrew word translated "troubler" is *'āḵar.* It literally means to roil, or to make muddy by stirring, water; to trouble, disturb, and stir things up.[1] Ahab was accusing Elijah of being the source of all the trouble, the root of the problem, and the one to blame for all that had been happening. And while Elijah had definitely been stirring some things up and would shortly stir them up even more, it wasn't to muddy the waters. Elijah had come to bring clarity, to bring truth, to cleanse, and to restore. It was Ahab who had muddied the waters, along with his wife Jezebel, with their idolatry and all the other forms of wickedness they were committing and encouraging in Israel.

This often happens with people who are walking in the spirit and power of Elijah. They are accused of being troublemakers—of stirring things up with negative consequences. They are accused of being the source of all the problems. But when Elijah prophets are speaking the truth of the Word with power and boldness, they are stirring things up to bring clarity, wholeness, and healing; to turn the hearts of people back to the Lord; and to bring people to the source of living water. The water of the Word that washes us clean isn't dirty, muddy, turbulent, and full of debris; it is clean, clear, calm, and refreshing, and it will wash you inside and out the way no other water ever could.

When people are confronted with their own sin, they often try to point the finger at someone else to take the focus off themselves. If they can get people to believe that the prophet is the problem, then they can dismiss any conviction they are feeling. And if they can dismiss the nudge in their spirit, then they don't have to change. They don't have to repent. Trying to shift the blame is an act of pride.

Modern-day prophets who faithfully speak the truth and proclaim God's Word may encounter opposition, resistance, or accusations of being disruptive or causing trouble. This can arise when their prophetic utterances confront systems of injustice, expose unrighteousness, or call for repentance and change in a society or within the church.

Prophets in this generation often carry a burden to address issues such as social injustice, moral decline, spiritual apathy, and the compromise of biblical truth. They challenge the status quo, calling for a return to God's standards and the pursuit of righteousness. Their messages may unsettle the comfortable and confront the complacent, leading to accusations of being troublemakers or disturbers of the peace.

However, it is important to discern that being labeled a "troubler" does not diminish the validity or importance of the prophetic voice. Rather, it emphasizes that the prophetic ministry, when faithfully carried out, often disrupts and challenges the prevailing systems and mindsets that are contrary to God's truth.

Modern-day prophets must remain steadfast and unwavering in their commitment to speak the truth in love, regardless of the opposition they face. They must rely on the discernment and wisdom of the Holy Spirit to navigate through accusations and adversity, always aligning their messages with the heart and Word of God.

The application of being a "troubler" to modern-day prophets calls for prophetic voices to courageously speak out against injustice, unrighteousness, and moral compromise, even when it is uncomfortable or unpopular. It emphasizes the need for prophets to remain firmly rooted in God's truth, trusting in His guidance and standing as advocates for righteousness and transformation in their respective spheres of influence.

As with the prophets of old, being a "troubler" in this context means embracing the prophetic mandate to challenge and disrupt systems that oppose God's will, all while seeking the restoration and redemption that His truth and love bring to individuals, communities, and nations.

When Ahab accused Elijah of troubling Israel, Elijah

responded right back with the truth: "I have not troubled Israel, but you and your father's house have, in that you have forsaken the commandments of the LORD and have followed the Baals" (1 Kings 18:18). Elijah didn't pull any punches. He recognized what the real problem was, and it was the pervasive idolatry in Israel because of Ahab. But because Ahab was trying to point the finger at Elijah, it was time to not only speak the truth but also demonstrate the truth.

SHOWDOWN

Elijah told Ahab to "send and gather all Israel to me on Mount Carmel, the four hundred and fifty prophets of Baal, and the four hundred prophets of Asherah, who eat at Jezebel's table" (1 Kings 18:19). He was ready to demonstrate that the Lord is God, and he wanted all of Israel to witness it. He wasn't going to leave the door open for Ahab, Jezebel, or any of the false prophets to twist the truth. He was ready to take on 850 false prophets, and he wanted an audience so that the hearts of the people could be turned back to the Lord.

When the people first gathered on Mount Carmel was when Elijah asked that key question: "How long will you falter between two opinions? If the LORD is God, follow Him; but if Baal, follow him" (1 Kings 18:21).

In this present generation, a cry resounds from the heavens, echoing the words of 1 Kings 18:21, "How long will you falter between two opinions?" This cry pierces through the noise and distractions of our time, challenging the church and individuals to examine the state of their hearts and make a resolute choice.

The cry speaks to the prevailing issue of spiritual compromise and divided loyalty. In a world filled with conflicting ideologies, the church and believers often find themselves wavering, straddling the line between the truth of God's Word and the allure of worldly influences. It is a call to wholeheartedly embrace the truths of God's kingdom and reject the deceptive lures of the world.

In this cry, heaven implores the church to shed its complacency, its lukewarmness, and its inclination toward compromise. This cry is a reminder that the Lord desires unwavering commitment, absolute surrender, and undivided devotion from His people.

The cry from heaven challenges the church to confront the idols and false beliefs that have crept into our lives. It calls us to renounce any allegiance to worldly ideologies, false gods, or sinful practices. It urges us to stand firm on the foundation of God's truth, refusing to be swayed by the shifting tides of popular opinion or cultural relativism.

This cry beckons us to embrace radical discipleship, making an unequivocal choice to follow Jesus Christ with our whole being. It calls for a steadfast commitment to live out the principles of His kingdom, even when faced with opposition or persecution.

As we respond to this cry from heaven, we are invited into a deeper relationship with God, where our hearts align with His heart, our minds are renewed by His Word, and our actions reflect His character. We become ambassadors of His truth, shining lights in a darkened world, and heralds of His redemptive message.

May this cry serve as a wake-up call to the church and individuals alike, urging us to wholeheartedly embrace God's truth, reject compromise, and walk in unwavering devotion. Let us heed this heavenly cry, for in doing so we will witness transformation, revival, and the manifest presence of God in our midst.

When the people on Mount Carmel didn't say a word in response to Elijah's question, it just confirmed to Elijah what the Lord had been showing him: the hearts of the people had turned from the Lord and were hardened against Him. So Elijah laid down the parameters of the showdown:

> I alone am left a prophet of the LORD; but Baal's prophets are four hundred and fifty men. Therefore let them give us two bulls; and let them choose one bull for themselves, cut it in pieces, and lay it on the wood, but put no fire under it; and I will prepare the other bull, and lay it on the wood, but put no fire under it. Then you call on the name of your gods, and I will call on the name of the LORD; and the God who answers by fire, He is God.
>
> —1 KINGS 18:22–24

The people agreed that it was a good test, a good way to demonstrate who was really God. Elijah let the prophets of Baal go first. They prepared the bull and leaped around the altar, calling out to Baal to hear them for hours, but nothing happened. Elijah started to mock them, telling them to shout louder—maybe Baal was busy or out for a walk or taking a nap. The response of the prophets of Baal was to cry even louder and to "cut themselves, as was their custom, with knives and lances, until the blood gushed out on them" (1 Kings 18:28). But the result was only silence. Despite their most intense efforts, no fire fell.

Then it was Elijah's turn. He called the people to him, and the first thing he did was repair the broken-down altar of the Lord. The Hebrew word translated "broken down" lets us know that the people of Israel had fallen so far away from the Lord that the altar wasn't just missing a stone or two—it had been pulled down, broken into pieces, destroyed, and utterly ruined.[2]

Rebuilding the broken altars of worship is part of walking in the spirit and power of Elijah. It is a call to the children of God to return to the worship of the one true God and reject idolatry. It is a reminder of who is really the Lord of all the earth and the only One deserving of our praise.

But Elijah didn't just rebuild the altar—he made it personal for the children of Israel. He took twelve stones, one for each of the tribes of Israel, and used them to build the altar in the name of the Lord. It wasn't just any altar; it was *their* altar, the one they should have been worshipping at all along. It must have reminded the people of another twelve stones, the ones that were taken from the Jordan River as the Israelites entered the Promised Land after forty years of wandering in the wilderness. One man from each tribe had chosen a stone from the river, and Joshua had set them up as a visual reminder of what the Lord had done for them:

> That this may be a sign among you when your children ask in time to come, saying, "What do these stones mean to you?" Then you shall answer them that the waters of the Jordan were cut off before the ark of the covenant of the LORD; when it crossed over the Jordan, the waters of the Jordan were cut off. And these stones shall be for a memorial to the children of Israel forever.
> —JOSHUA 4:6–7

Just as the people who crossed the Jordan on dry land knew they were represented in twelve stones, reminding them of the wonders and miracles of the Lord, the people of Israel gathered on Mount Carmel knew they were represented in the rebuilt altar.

Elijah didn't stop at rebuilding the altar. He dug a trench around the altar big enough to hold several gallons of water. He then had the people fill four water pots and pour them on the altar three times. The sacrifice and the wood were soaked, and even the trench around the altar was full of water. Elijah wanted to make sure it was 100 percent clear there was no way a human could set fire to the sacrifice. He also offered to God the most precious commodity in a drought, which was water.

Then it was time.

> Elijah the prophet came near and said, "LORD God of
> Abraham, Isaac, and Israel, let it be known this day that
> You are God in Israel and I am Your servant, and that
> I have done all these things at Your word. Hear me, O
> LORD, hear me, that this people may know that You are
> the LORD God, and that You have turned their hearts
> back to You again."
> Then the fire of the LORD fell and consumed the
> burnt sacrifice, and the wood and the stones and the
> dust, and it licked up the water that was in the trench.
> Now when all the people saw it, they fell on their faces;
> and they said, "The LORD, He is God! The LORD, He
> is God!"
>
> —1 KINGS 18:36–39

The Lord answered by fire. The fire of the Lord consumed
everything—the sacrifice, the wood, the water, and even the
stones of the altar. The Lord made it clear: He is God.

SPIRITUAL EXCHANGE

Altars are places of spiritual exchange, whether demonic or
godly. The altar of the Lord is the place where you meet God.
God is at the center; He is the focus. The altar is a place where
God comes. It is an altar of praise and worship to the true and
living God. When you come to the altar, you encounter God,
and thus it is a place of transformation.

The altar is also the place where sacrifices are offered up.
We no longer have to sacrifice animals on the altar of the
Lord because Jesus' sacrifice on the cross at Calvary covered
all our sin once and for all. But we can still make a sacrifice
at the altar of the Lord. We can offer up a sacrifice of praise.
Hebrews 13:15 says, "Therefore by Him let us continually offer

the sacrifice of praise to God, that is, the fruit of our lips, giving thanks to His name."

We can also offer up a sacrifice of thanksgiving to the Lord through our actions, through the way we bless others, and by doing justly, loving mercy, and walking humbly with the Lord. Hebrews continues by saying, "But do not forget to do good and to share, for with such sacrifices God is well pleased" (v. 16). The Lord loves it when we share His love with others in word and deed. But the sacrifice that pleases Him the most is when we offer up ourselves and become living sacrifices to the glory of the Lord.

> I beseech you therefore, brethren, by the mercies of God, that you present your bodies a living sacrifice, holy, acceptable to God, which is your reasonable service. And do not be conformed to this world, but be transformed by the renewing of your mind, that you may prove what is that good and acceptable and perfect will of God.
>
> —ROMANS 12:1–2

This is the spiritual exchange at the altar of the Lord: we offer up ourselves as living sacrifices, following the Word of the Lord and seeking and carrying out His will for our lives, and He transforms us. He makes us more and more like Jesus, the author and finisher of our faith. At the altar we encounter the glory of the Lord, and it changes us: "But we all, with unveiled face, beholding as in a mirror the glory of the Lord, are being transformed into the same image from glory to glory, just as by the Spirit of the Lord" (2 Cor. 3:18).

What is even more precious is that we can work together, as the body of Christ, to build an altar of praise.

> Coming to Him as to a living stone, rejected indeed by men, but chosen by God and precious, you also, as

living stones, are being built up a spiritual house, a holy priesthood, to offer up spiritual sacrifices acceptable to God through Jesus Christ....But you are a chosen generation, a royal priesthood, a holy nation, His own special people, that you may proclaim the praises of Him who called you out of darkness into His marvelous light; who once were not a people but are now the people of God, who had not obtained mercy but now have obtained mercy.

—1 PETER 2:4–5, 9–10

When you are moving in the spirit and power of Elijah, you will be rejected by men. But that is OK—you have been chosen by God, and you are precious in His sight. You are a living stone, one of many that is being used to build the kingdom of God in the earth. You have been called out of the darkness into His marvelous light, covered by His mercy, and redeemed by His grace so that you might share the love, grace, mercy, and forgiveness of the Lord God Almighty with the people who have turned their hearts away from Him. You have been called to be a living sacrifice, not giving in to the fear of man but rather speaking the truth with boldness and in love to call this generation to repent and return.

When you come to the altar of worship and your heart is in the right place, when you come to the altar to worship the Lord in spirit and in truth, the spiritual exchange takes place. You come with your worship. In return, you get the blessings of God. You get the favor of God. You get peace. You get joy. You get love. You get mercy, grace, and forgiveness. You get freedom. You get hope. You go from glory to glory as the Lord changes you to make you more and more like Jesus. And best of all, you get to be in relationship with the King of kings and Lord of lords, the Creator of all the earth, the Most High God, the Anointed One, the Holy One, the Lord who provides, the

Lord who protects, the Lord who saves, the Lord who heals, the Lord who redeems.

When the false prophets were crying out to Baal as they danced around the altar they had built, they said, "O Baal, hear us!" (1 Kings 18:26). The Hebrew word for *hear* used in the passage means to eye, to heed, to pay attention, and to answer.[3] Elijah used the same word when he prayed to the Lord. And isn't that what we need from God? We need Him to see us, we need Him to hear us and listen to our cries for help, we need Him to pay attention to us and understand us, and we need Him to answer us when we call on Him. And the true and living God does all those things.

But when you are looking to a false god, to an idol, to do all those things, you will be disappointed. A false god—no matter how wonderful it seems—can never take the place of the Lord. He is the One who created you, who knows you personally and intimately, who has a good plan for your life to give you a future and a hope, who works all things together for your good, and who loves you far beyond what you can even imagine. When you look to a false god to fulfill your needs, all you get is disappointment, heartache, bondage, hopelessness, and silence.

When you choose to worship at the altar of an idol, instead of blessings you bring curses upon yourself. So many people are blind to it and think there is nothing wrong with it, but they are being deceived. Satan is the father of lies (John 8:44). He comes to steal, kill, and destroy (John 10:10). He may make your idols pleasant for a time, but in the long run they will lead to your destruction. The enemy will reward you for a season, but it is a temporal benefit from selling your soul to the devil.

Instead of favor you get failure. Instead of peace you get turmoil. Instead of joy you get sorrow. Instead of love you get a heart full of hate and fear. Instead of mercy, grace, and forgiveness you get condemnation and judgment. Instead of freedom you get bondage. Instead of hope you get hopelessness. Instead of becoming more and more like Jesus, you become more and more like the world and the ruler of this world. And worst of all, you miss out on being in relationship with the Lord. That is the spiritual exchange when you go to the altars of idols, when you worship false gods, when you give place to the demonic, when you have a heart full of idolatry.

The church today has come to a place where we have a lot of idol worship. An idol is anything you put ahead of your worship of the Lord. Any god other than Jesus is a false god. If you are not worshipping the true and living God, you are worshipping idols. We have built personal altars to our personal idols, to people and things and systems rather than to the Lord God Almighty. Money and consumerism are very common idols. Pride is another common one. But the truth is that God will judge our pride. The Word says, "Pride goes before destruction, and a haughty spirit before a fall" (Prov. 16:18). It also warns that if you are "puffed up with pride [you can] fall into the same condemnation as the devil" (1 Tim. 3:6).

People want power without God, but real power comes only from Him. The power the world offers is a snare. Think of all the things people sacrifice to obtain worldly power—their families, their character, their health, the well-being of others, their relationships with the Lord… The cost is great, and power apart from the Lord will never bring you joy or peace.

People today have turned to all sorts of false gods, idols, and the occult. A 2018 *Newsweek* article reported that an estimated 1.5 million Americans practice witchcraft.[4] To put that in perspective, Hawaii is ranked forty out of fifty states in terms of population, and it only has 1.4 million people. That means the witch population is greater than the population of eleven different states.

The deception related to these practices is real. In a recent article in *Essence*, a witch drew parallels between witchcraft and Christianity, saying, "A conjure and a prayer are one and the same."[5] Let me be clear: witchcraft is demonic. (See Deuteronomy 18:10–14.)

DECEPTION IN THE CHURCH

All kinds of deception is making its way into the church. People are being seduced by doctrines of demons. There are books connecting Christianity to witchcraft, chakras, tarot cards, astrology, and many other demonic and occult practices. This shouldn't be the case, but when the church is no longer grounded in the Word of the God, when believers start to pick and choose Bible verses that apply to their lives, when the shepherds are no longer warning the sheep about the dangers they are facing, it is all too easy to be deceived.

Don't think the actions of the prophets of Baal have no relevance today. One of the results of their idol worship was self-harm: "So they cried aloud, and cut themselves, as was their custom, with knives and lances, until the blood gushed out on them" (1 Kings 18:28). As our culture gets further and further from the Lord, the prevalence of self-harm is increasing. One study reported that 7.6 percent of *third graders* in the study had engaged in non-suicidal self-injury (NSSI). We are talking about eight-year-olds cutting themselves. The percentage of ninth graders involved in such behavior was even higher, at 12.7 percent.[6] Lifetime rates of NSSI among teenagers and young adults is between 15 and 20 percent.[7] Emergency room visits related to self-inflicted injury among girls from ten to fourteen years old increased 18.8 percent from 2009 to 2015.[8] It is heartbreaking.

That is why it isn't enough to tear down the demonic altars and leave the space empty, for it will end up even worse than before. (See Matthew 12:43–45.)

Elijahs need to rebuild the altars of the Lord.

REBUILDING THE ALTAR OF GOD

Rebuilding the altars of the Lord and executing the justice of the Lord are both part of the assignment of those walking in the spirit and power of Elijah.

> Then Elijah said to all the people, "Come near to me." So all the people came near to him. And he repaired the altar of the LORD that was broken down.
> —1 KINGS 18:30

Elijah invited the people to come near and witness. He desired the people to personally observe his actions. He demonstrated deep respect for the altar of the Lord. Not only did the prophets of Baal disregard the significance of the altar, but God's people lacked understanding of its true meaning. Moreover, the altar required restoration, as it had been treated with disrespect by the followers of Baal. The mention of the twelve tribes served as a reminder of the people's glorious ancestry. They were distinct from other nations, chosen as God's covenant people and treasured possession. Their heritage was sacred, tracing back to the time of Moses and the revered patriarchs— Abraham, Isaac, and Jacob.

In the context of modern-day Elijahs or prophets, rebuilding the altar of God symbolizes a restoration and revival of true worship, spiritual fervor, and a return to the foundational truths of the faith. Here are some ways in which modern-day Elijahs can participate in rebuilding the altar of God:

- Proclaiming the truth—Modern-day Elijahs are called to boldly proclaim the truth of God's Word, confronting falsehood and deception. They challenge cultural norms that deviate from God's standards.

- Reviving passionate worship—Elijahs of today inspire and lead others into heartfelt and passionate worship of God. They encourage a revival of worship that goes beyond mere rituals or routine so that believers offer their genuine love, adoration, and surrender to God.

- Prayer and intercession—Modern-day Elijahs understand the power of prayer and intercession in rebuilding the altar of God. They fervently seek God's face, standing in the gap for individuals, communities, and nations.

- Confronting idolatry—Just as Elijah confronted the prophets of Baal, modern-day Elijahs challenge the idolatrous systems that exist today. They expose the false gods and counterfeit beliefs that have crept into society and the church.

- Healing and restoration—Elijahs in this generation engage in ministries of healing, deliverance, and restoration. They help rebuild broken lives and bring individuals back to a place of wholeness and surrender to God.

- Modeling a life of holiness—Modern-day Elijahs strive to live lives of holiness and integrity, serving as examples for others to follow. They inspire others to rebuild their own personal altars of consecration and devotion to God.

Through these actions and attitudes, modern-day Elijahs prophetically participate in rebuilding the altar of God. They play a vital role in restoring the foundations of faith, revival, and true worship, leading individuals and the church to experience a renewed and vibrant relationship with God.

CONFRONTING IDOLATRY

Confronting idolatry in the twenty-first-century church involves addressing the various forms of misplaced worship and devotion that can subtly infiltrate our lives and communities. Here are some aspects of confronting idolatry in the modern-day church:

- Exposing false beliefs and teachings—The modern church must discern and address false teachings and ideologies that can lead to idolatrous practices. This includes confronting teachings that distort the true nature of God, compromise biblical truths, or elevate human wisdom above God's Word.

- Challenging materialism and consumerism—In a consumer-driven culture, the church must confront the idolatry of material possessions, wealth, and consumerism. This involves a shift in perspective from pursuing material gain to embracing a lifestyle of stewardship, generosity, and contentment.

- Addressing the idol of self—Self-centeredness and self-fulfillment can become idols in the modern church. We must encourage believers to deny themselves, take up their crosses, and live lives focused on God's purposes and the needs of others.

- Confronting the idol of success and celebrity—The church is susceptible to idolizing success, fame, and the pursuit of personal recognition.

Addressing this idolatry means valuing humility, servant leadership, and the exaltation of God rather than seeking personal acclaim or building platforms for self-promotion.

- Encouraging true worship and relationship with God—The twenty-first-century church must place a renewed emphasis on authentic worship and cultivate a deep, intimate relationship with God. In an atmosphere of heartfelt worship, God's presence is revered, His Word is honored, and lives are transformed.

- Emphasizing the supremacy of Christ—We must remind believers of the supremacy of Jesus Christ and that He alone is the way, the truth, and the life. No other person, ideology, or object can replace His central place in our lives.

- Cultivating discipleship and spiritual formation—The church must prioritize discipleship and intentional spiritual formation. This involves teaching believers to recognize and address idolatrous tendencies, develop a strong foundation in biblical truth, and foster a lifestyle of ongoing transformation in Christ.

It is important to confront idolatry with love, grace, and humility. By addressing these areas of idolatry, the modern church can create an environment that fosters a deep love for God, where His presence is exalted and His glory is magnified.

Modern-day Elijahs display unwavering faith and trust in God, believing in His power to bring about the impossible. They operate in the supernatural, moving in signs, wonders, and miracles as they release the transformative power of the Holy Spirit.

They understand the authority they carry, and like Elijah, they demonstrate discernment and prophetic accuracy. They are sensitive to the times and seasons, revealing hidden truths, bringing clarity, and releasing strategic prophetic words that align with God's purposes.

Modern-day prophets with the spirit and power of Elijah are called to boldly confront the prevailing spiritual climate, expose idolatry, release the power of the Holy Spirit, speak truth with accuracy, intercede fervently, rebuild the altar of true worship, and bring forth transformation and revival in their spheres of influence. They play a vital role in preparing the way for the coming of the Lord and the establishment of His kingdom on earth.

The Word says, "The hour is coming, and now is, when the true worshipers will worship the Father in spirit and truth; for the Father is seeking such to worship Him. God is Spirit, and those who worship Him must worship in spirit and truth" (John 4:23–24). The time for giving lip service to the Lord or worshipping Him out of a sense of tradition or obligation with no heart behind it is over. God wants pure worship. He wants the hearts, voices, and hands of those who love Him and seek to obey Him lifted to Him in praise. He wants living sacrifices, living stones. He wants us to worship Him in word and deed. He wants us to worship Him in spirit and truth.

When Elijah rebuilt the altar, it was the first step in calling the children of Israel back to real worship. They had fallen far, but the showdown on Mount Carmel reminded them of the truth. It turned their hearts back to the living God, and they immediately began to worship, falling on their faces and declaring the truth: "The Lord, He is God! The Lord, He is God!" (1 Kings 18:39).

But Elijah's assignment also included carrying out the justice of the Lord. After the showdown was over, Elijah executed all the prophets of Baal. In Old Testament times, justice was executed quite differently, which is why Elijah killed the prophets of Baal. But today we have the power of the Holy Spirit. We have the ability to cast out demons just as Jesus did. So we execute justice not by killing people who are possessed or oppressed by demons but by casting out the demons and sending them wherever Jesus tells them to go.

Because of Jesus, mercy triumphs over judgment. But we do have to confront false prophets and demonic spirits—such as the Jezebel spirit or the religious spirit—with the Word of God. We need to be the voices crying out, "The word of our God stands forever" (Isa. 40:8). Isaiah 58:1 says, "Cry aloud, spare not; lift up your voice like a trumpet; tell My people their transgression, and the house of Jacob their sins." Elijahs need to be crying out with voices like trumpets to call the people to turn back to the Lord.

God will move in miracles, signs, and wonders to judge demonic spirits but also to uncover the deception at work and to cause the hearts of His people to turn. Through the power of deliverance, principalities are judged. Elijahs exact the justice of God through prayer, through confronting idolatry, through confronting false doctrines, through preaching, and through miracles, signs, and wonders.

Elijahs have to bind the strong man and cast those spirits out (Matt. 12:29). It is time to set the captives free.

> Is this not the fast that I have chosen: to loose the bonds of wickedness, to undo the heavy burdens, to let the oppressed go free, and that you break every yoke?
> —ISAIAH 58:6

> Therefore if the Son makes you free, you shall be free indeed.
> —JOHN 8:36

So many people are lost and hurting because they have turned away from the Lord. But God still loves them, and He wants them to return to Him. He is seeking them to bring them back, to heal them, to restore them, to deliver them, to set them free from bondage, and to bless them once again so they know deep in their hearts that they are children of God.

> For thus says the Lord GOD: "Indeed I Myself will search for My sheep and seek them out. As a shepherd seeks out his flock on the day he is among his scattered sheep, so will I seek out My sheep and deliver them from all the places where they were scattered on a cloudy and dark day....I will seek what was lost and bring back what was driven away, bind up the broken and strengthen what was sick....I will make a covenant of peace with them.... Thus they shall know that I, the LORD their God, am with them, and they, the house of Israel, are My people," says the Lord GOD.
>   —EZEKIEL 34:11–12, 16, 25, 30

God is getting ready to knock down every demonic idol. But guess who He is going to use? The spirit of Elijah turns hearts back to the Lord, but it also destroys hedonism. Elijah was called to root out and completely destroy the evil in the land, and the Elijah prophets of today have the same call. Let the preachers of righteousness arise. Let the demonic altars fall. Let the altars of the Lord be built up with living stones. And let the children of God worship Him in spirit and in truth.

Chapter 7

The Power of
Persistent Prayer

THE INTERCESSORY ASPECT of the Elijah anointing is pivotal to accomplishing the work this prophet is sent to do. The prayers of Elijah prophets are meant to move heaven and shake the earth. This level of powerful prayer does not come without the prophet having been set apart and refined at Cherith—their wilderness experience. The time hidden away in the wilderness develops the foundational relationship with the Lord that is necessary for Elijah prophets to hear clearly from Him and then pray for His will to happen in the earth.

Elijah, with his prophetic insight, heard the sound of rain even before any physical indication of its arrival. This illustrates how prophets have the ability to perceive what is yet to manifest in the spiritual realm and bring it into existence on the earth. This revelation serves as a driving force for persistence in prayer.

Through their intimate connection with God, prophets can discern the plans and purposes He has ordained. They catch a glimpse of the future and God's intentions for His people and the world. This insight enables them to pray with unwavering faith, aligning their prayers with God's will and partnering with Him to bring about His desired outcomes.

When prophets hear the sound of rain in the spirit, it ignites a sense of urgency and perseverance in prayer. They understand that although the manifestation may not be immediately visible, they have a divine mandate to persist in seeking God's intervention and bringing forth His promises. Their prayers become a powerful catalyst for transformation and the fulfillment of God's purposes on earth.

The prophetic impetus to persist in prayer comes from the deep conviction that God is faithful to His Word. Prophets recognize that their prayers have the potential to shift spiritual atmospheres, dismantle spiritual opposition, and release God's blessings and breakthroughs into the natural realm.

This understanding of the spiritual realm and the role of prayer propels prophets to press on, even when circumstances seem bleak or contrary. They draw strength from their prophetic insight, knowing that God's plans are unchanging and that their persistent prayers align with His divine timeline.

Prophets have the unique ability to see what is waiting to exist in the spirit realm and bring it into manifestation on the earth. This revelation serves as a catalyst for persistence in prayer, fueling their unwavering faith and commitment to intercede until God's promises are fulfilled. Prophets understand the power of their prayers and press on, knowing that God is faithful and that their persistent prayers align with His divine purposes.

Elijah's declaration of no rain (1 Kings 17:1) and subsequent command for rain (1 Kings 18:41–42) was indeed a profound battle that showcased the sovereignty of God over the elements and the clash between the true God of Israel and the false gods worshipped in that time.

His declaration of no rain was not merely a weather prediction; it was a prophetic proclamation that revealed the authority and power of the God he served. By declaring a drought, Elijah was challenging the prevailing belief in Baal, a Canaanite deity often associated with controlling rain and fertility. In this act, Elijah was confronting the false god's supposed dominion over nature.

Elijah's dramatic challenge on Mount Carmel (1 Kings 18) further emphasized this spiritual battle. He set up a showdown between himself and the prophets of Baal to prove once and for all who truly controlled the elements. The prophets of Baal fervently called upon their god to send fire, but their efforts were in vain. In contrast, Elijah's single prayer to the God of Israel resulted in a consuming fire descending from heaven, demonstrating the true divine authority over nature.

When Elijah declared, "There is the sound of abundance of rain" (1 Kings 18:41), he not only announced the physical end of the drought but also symbolized the spiritual victory of the true God over the false gods. His subsequent prayer for rain and the immediate response of a heavy downpour highlighted God's sovereignty and Elijah's connection with the divine.

In a broader sense, Elijah's actions mirrored the ongoing spiritual battle between the one true God and the idolatry that had infiltrated the land. Through these events, God revealed His supremacy over nature and His willingness to vindicate His name before the people of Israel.

This narrative holds significance for the modern-day church as well. It reminds believers that God's authority extends over all creation, and He remains in control of even the most fundamental elements of the world. It encourages us to place our trust in the Almighty, knowing that He can bring about miraculous intervention and transformation in the face of seemingly insurmountable challenges.

Elijah's bold stance against false gods also serves as a call to confront and challenge the idols and false beliefs of our own time. Just as Elijah stood firm in his declaration of God's sovereignty, the modern-day church is called to boldly proclaim the truth of the gospel and resist the influences of secularism, materialism, and other forms of idolatry.

In essence, Elijah's declaration and the subsequent battle over rain highlight the supremacy of the one true God and His authority over all aspects of creation, including the elements. It serves as a reminder that God is always in control and that He will vindicate His name in the face of challenges to His sovereignty.

SHAMELESS PERSISTENCE

This is a critical time in history. Moral depravity, physical and financial hardship, and spiritual decline have left people impoverished in numerous ways. Gross darkness covers the face of the earth. Many people may look at the current state of the world and think there is no hope, that all is lost, and that the downward cycle will just continue, so everyone might as well give in to it. But that is a lie from the enemy. He is doing everything in his power to steal, kill, and destroy hope. But there is hope—in Jesus. The Lord promised in Psalm 2:8 that He would give Jesus the nations for His inheritance and the ends of the earth for His possession. The nations belong to Jesus. It is time for those walking in the spirit and power of Elijah to start interceding on behalf of the nations so they can be returned to their rightful owner. But Elijah prophets must persist in prayer.

According to *Merriam-Webster, persist* means "to go on resolutely…to be insistent in the repetition or pressing of an utterance."[1] Persistence in prayer is a characteristic of the spirit and power of Elijah. Those with the Elijah anointing do not give up after praying for something one time. Rather, they pray again and again, going on resolutely and pressing their case with the Lord until they see their prayers come to fruition.

Elijahs pray for the will of God to be manifested in the earth. It is a spiritual discipline they develop in their Cherith time.

Once they cultivate that skill, they ask the Lord for things based on His love for them and all His children. God is our heavenly Father, and He loves to give good gifts to His children (Luke 11:13). That enables Elijah prophets to pray for revival, revelation, reformation, redemption, renewal, repentance, return, and restoration. They can intercede for spiritual awakening on behalf of their families, their communities, their cities, their nations, and the world. The earth, all its fullness, and those who dwell in it are the Lord's (Ps. 24:1), which means that our intercession can influence the whole earth. We don't have to sit idly by and watch our nation descend further and further into idolatry. We can ask God to intervene—and He will.

After the showdown on Mount Carmel, Elijah told Ahab, "Go up, eat and drink; for there is the sound of abundance of rain" (1 Kings 18:41). Keep in mind that there had been a drought for three years—because Elijah prayed for one. Ahab had seen enough to take Elijah at his word, so he went up to eat and drink, just as Elijah said.

Elijah went to the top of the mountain and bowed down to pray. He then told his servant to go look toward the sea. The servant looked and reported that he didn't see anything. So Elijah told him to look again. And again the servant didn't see anything. This happened again and again. It was only after Elijah had prayed the seventh time that the servant said, "There is a cloud, as small as a man's hand, rising out of the sea!" (1 Kings 18:44). The drought was finally coming to an end. However, even though Elijah knew his assignment, even though he knew the drought would end, even though he was praying at the unction of the Holy Spirit, he still had to pray seven times before it happened. He still had to persist in prayer.

When the widow of Zarephath's son died, Elijah knew what his assignment was. He knew what the Lord was calling him to do. But Elijah cried out to the Lord for the life of the child three times before God brought the boy back to life. Once again, Elijah had to persist in prayer.

Both times Elijah didn't doubt his assignment. He didn't doubt the word the Lord had spoken to him. He kept on praying until he saw the answer.

When God doesn't answer right away, the enemy will try to make you doubt. He will try to make you doubt your calling, your assignment, and your ability to hear the Lord correctly. Yet when you are moving in the spirit and power of Elijah, you can't let the enemy's seeds of doubt take root in your heart and mind. When the enemy tries to plant a seed of doubt, rise up in faith and keep on praying.

Jesus told this parable:

> There was in a certain city a judge who did not fear God nor regard man. Now there was a widow in that city; and she came to him, saying, "Get justice for me from my adversary." And he would not for a while; but afterward he said within himself, "Though I do not fear God nor regard man, yet because this widow troubles me I will avenge her, lest by her continual coming she weary me."
>
> —Luke 18:2–5

The stated purpose of the parable was "that men always ought to pray and not lose heart" (Luke 18:1). It is all too easy to give up when our prayers aren't answered the first time we pray them, but we need to keep praying. In the parable, even an unjust judge was willing to answer the poor widow because of her persistence. However, the Lord is not an unjust judge. Psalm 9:8 says, "He shall judge the world in righteousness, and He shall administer judgment for the peoples in uprightness." Other psalms add that He will judge "the peoples with His truth" and "with equity" (Ps. 96:13; 98:9). Justice and righteousness are the foundation of His throne, and mercy and truth go before Him

(Ps. 89:14). On top of that, God is a good Father. Given all those things, we can trust that when we persist in prayer, He will answer according to His will and His timing.

Many of us are familiar with Luke 11:9–10: "So I say to you, ask, and it will be given to you; seek, and you will find; knock, and it will be opened to you. For everyone who asks receives, and he who seeks finds, and to him who knocks it will be opened." But before Jesus said to ask, seek, and knock, He set the stage with an illustration:

> And He said to them, "Which of you shall have a friend, and go to him at midnight and say to him, 'Friend, lend me three loaves; for a friend of mine has come to me on his journey, and I have nothing to set before him'; and he will answer from within and say, 'Do not trouble me; the door is now shut, and my children are with me in bed; I cannot rise and give to you'? I say to you, though he will not rise and give to him because he is his friend, yet because of his persistence he will rise and give him as many as he needs.
>
> —Luke 11:5–8

When we read the passage in English, we lose some of the meaning that is clear in the Greek. The word translated "persistence" is *anaideia*, and it means importunity, or being over-the-top persistent in seeking what you want or need.[2] *Anaideia* comes from two Greek words, one meaning shame and the other being a negative particle. Put the two words together and it means without shame. In fact, one Bible version translates the word as "shameless persistence" (Luke 11:8, AMPC).

The Greek also gives insight into what Jesus was saying to do. The verbs *ask*, *seek*, and *knock* in verse 9 are in the present active imperative tense. That means they are commands intended to be an ongoing process. It's like when the doctor tells you to exercise. He isn't telling you to walk one lap around the block and you're done, no need to exercise ever again. He is telling you to keep exercising on a regular basis. It's the same thing in the passage in Luke—Jesus was saying to ask and keep on asking, to seek and keep on seeking, to knock and keep on knocking.

When we persist, we receive. When we persist in seeking, we find. When we persist in knocking, doors open. Persistence is the key. And again, because God is a good Father who delights in giving good gifts to His children, we can trust that He will answer. We can trust that He will give us exactly what we need. We can trust that He will work all things together for our good. We can trust that He will do whatever is necessary to help us fulfill our assignments on the earth—He will send rain or dry it up, raise the dead, send miraculous provision, heal the sick, let His fire fall, move mountains, calm a storm, or do whatever it takes to call His people to return to Him.

When you are walking in the spirit and power of Elijah, you must persist in prayer. If we are going to see revival, reformation, and restoration in our nation, we must have fixed determination to see the goodness of God in the land of the living. We need to be persistent, insistent, and enduring in prayer.

PRAYER AND INTERCESSION

Outside of the Old Testament and the Gospels, Elijah is only mentioned by name twice in the Bible, once in Romans and once in the Book of James—and both mentions are in the context of prayer.

Romans 11:2 says, "Or do you not know what the Scripture says of Elijah, how he pleads with God...?" The Greek word for *pleads* means to confer with, to entreat, to meet someone for the purpose of supplication, to pray, to plead, or to make intercession.[3] Elijah prophets are intercessors. They intercede with the Lord on behalf of others, entreating the Lord for favor or pleading with Him to act against the demonic forces at work in a situation. They persistently plead for the Lord's hand to move.

The other mention of Elijah is in a familiar passage:

> The effective, fervent prayer of a righteous man avails much. Elijah was a man with a nature like ours, and he prayed earnestly that it would not rain; and it did not rain on the land for three years and six months. And he prayed again, and the heaven gave rain, and the earth produced its fruit.
>
> —JAMES 5:16–19

Elijah's close connection with God allowed him to know the heart of God and receive His unction, which enabled Elijah to pray according to His will and know that the Lord would answer. He was a natural man with natural passions and inclinations, but God gave him an anointing to be persistent and to intercede on behalf of a nation.

Elijah had an unction from the Lord that gave him the resilience to persist until he saw results. He prayed earnestly with a sincere heart. He had confidence in the Lord. Because he had the unction of the Lord, he knew he was praying according to his assignment. Once we have our assignment from the Lord, it is our responsibility to pray earnestly and keep ourselves in the middle of God's will as we walk out our assignment and deliver the message the Lord has given us.

THE POWER OF RIGHTEOUSNESS

The Book of James refers to "the effective, fervent prayer of a righteous man" (Jas. 5:16). All those adjectives are important for the prayers of those walking in the spirit and power of Elijah. Righteousness is indeed a crucial aspect for prophets—and all believers—in their battle against the powers of darkness.

To effectively confront and overcome the powers of darkness, prophets must uphold righteousness as a foundational principle. Righteousness acts as both a protective shield and a source of spiritual authority. It establishes a firm moral and ethical foundation, aligning prophets with God's character and purposes.

By embracing righteousness, prophets demonstrate a commitment to living in accordance with God's commands and values. This includes integrity, honesty, purity, and a pursuit of justice and mercy. Such a lifestyle empowers prophets to walk in harmony with God, hear His voice clearly, and discern the strategies of the enemy.

The powers of darkness seek to undermine righteousness and exploit areas of compromise or unrighteousness. However, prophets who diligently pursue righteousness become fortified against the attacks of the enemy. Their righteous living acts as a deterrent, limiting the influence of demonic forces and exposing the works of darkness.

Moreover, righteousness serves as a source of spiritual authority for prophets. When their lives are characterized by righteousness, they possess a heightened ability to exercise the authority of God's kingdom. Their words and actions carry weight, and their prayers become potent weapons against the forces of evil.

It is important to note that righteousness is not a product of human effort alone. Prophets rely on the grace of God and the empowering work of the Holy Spirit to walk in righteousness. Through a deep and intimate relationship with God, prophets receive the enabling power to live righteously and combat the darkness that seeks to hinder God's purposes.

Righteousness is God's mark of distinction for true prophets. As prophets strive to live righteously, they align themselves with God's purposes, discern His leading, and become effective instruments in advancing His kingdom on earth.

You need to have a relationship with the Lord to make sure

your prayers are heard, but you also need to be walking before Him in righteousness. Isaiah 59:2 says, "But your iniquities have separated you from your God; and your sins have hidden His face from you, so that He will not hear." Psalm 66:18 says, "If I regard iniquity in my heart, the LORD will not hear." Unconfessed sin, especially habitual sin, puts a wall of separation between you and the Lord. That is why you need to deal with your sin. Be especially wary of any issues the Lord dealt with during your Cherith season. Don't let those issues come back and get a stronghold in your heart again. When you sin, repent immediately. Don't give the devil a foothold.

Unforgiveness is another shade of unrighteousness that can hinder your prayer. Jesus said, "And whenever you stand praying, if you have anything against anyone, forgive him, that your Father in heaven may also forgive you your trespasses" (Mark 11:25). A righteous man or woman needs to have a heart free from bitterness and unforgiveness. When you have the Elijah anointing, you will come under attack from others. But you must recognize that the devil is the one who is really behind the attack, and you need to forgive them. Don't let any seeds of bitterness grow in your heart, because bitter roots are hard to get rid of.

In James 5:16 "effective, fervent" is actually just one word in the Greek: *energeō*. It comes from the same root word from which we get the word *energy*, and it means to be active, to work, to be mighty, to be effectual, to be fervent.[4] In other words, it means you need to do something! Prayer is an active thing, not passive. When Elijah prophets pray, there is power in their prayers to get things done. They are fervent in their prayers, meaning they are zealous, earnest, and diligent. Their prayers are also effective, meaning that things happen when Elijah prophets pray.

As Elijah prophets, God has given us authority. We not only have the power to pray, but we also have the authority to pray because God has given us permission. When God has given you an assignment and the authority to carry it out, you need to exercise that authority. God gives us an anointing as prophets to contend earnestly until we see the answer.

POWER AND AUTHORITY WORK TOGETHER

Jesus said, "But you shall receive power when the Holy Spirit has come upon you; and you shall be witnesses to Me in Jerusalem, and in all Judea and Samaria, and to the end of the earth" (Acts 1:8). He also said, "Most assuredly, I say to you, he who believes in Me, the works that I do he will do also; and greater works than these he will do, because I go to My Father" (John 14:12), and, "Assuredly, I say to you, whatever you bind on earth will be bound in heaven, and whatever you loose on earth will be loosed in heaven" (Matt. 18:18). Jesus gave us power to do greater works by giving us the Holy Spirit, but He also gave us the authority to do those works. He gave us both power and authority—they work together.

However, if someone's power comes from the demonic realm instead of from the Lord, any authority they have is illegal. The Lord responds only to legal authority. The same is true of angels.

We must understand the difference between power and authority. In Luke 10:19, Jesus uses both the words *power* and *authority* to convey distinct aspects of His gift to His disciples. Understanding the difference between these terms can provide deeper insight into the verse.

Power, the Greek word *dunamis*, refers to the inherent strength, ability, or force that one possesses. In Luke 10:19, when Jesus says, "Behold, I give you the authority to trample on serpents and scorpions," the word *trample* indicates a physical act of domination or victory over enemies. The power Jesus imparts to His disciples is the supernatural ability or force to overcome and prevail over the attacks and schemes of the enemy. It is the power to perform miraculous acts and experience divine intervention.

Authority, the Greek word *exousia*,[5] refers to the delegated right or permission to exercise power or control over a particular domain. In the same verse, when Jesus says, "I give you the authority...over all the power of the enemy," He grants His disciples the authority to exercise dominion and rule over the forces of darkness. This authority comes from Jesus Himself, as He delegates His divine power to His disciples, empowering them to act on His behalf and in accordance with His will.

In essence, power represents inherent strength or force, while authority refers to the delegated right or permission to exercise that power. Jesus gives His disciples both the power to overcome and conquer the enemy and the authority to act in His name, carrying out His purposes.

It is important to note that the distinction between power and authority does not imply a separation or hierarchy between the two. Rather, they work in conjunction, with authority enabling the proper use and application of power. Through the power and authority given by Jesus, His disciples are equipped to confront and triumph over the forces of darkness and bring about the advancement of God's kingdom.

Even evil spirits know the difference between legal and illegal authority:

> Then some of the itinerant Jewish exorcists took it upon themselves to call the name of the Lord Jesus over those who had evil spirits, saying, "We exorcise you by the Jesus whom Paul preaches." Also there were seven sons of Sceva, a Jewish chief priest, who did so.
>
> And the evil spirit answered and said, "Jesus I know, and Paul I know; but who are you?" Then the man in whom the evil spirit was leaped on them, overpowered them, and prevailed against them, so that they fled out of that house naked and wounded.
>
> —ACTS 19:13–16

Elijah was a man just like us. He didn't have any special abilities that we don't have. Yet his prayers shut the heavens, opened them back up again, raised the dead, and called down fire from heaven. Elijah just stood before the Lord, and the Lord anointed him to carry out his assignment.

You have been chosen by God for this assignment, for this generation, for this season. Jeremiah 1:5 says, "Before I formed you in the womb I knew you; before you were born I sanctified you; I ordained you a prophet to the nations." Jesus said, "You did not choose Me, but I chose you and appointed you that you should go and bear fruit, and that your fruit should remain, that whatever you ask the Father in My name He may give you" (John 15:16). You have been chosen, and chosen ones chase after God. They grab hold like Jacob did when he wrestled with the Lord, and they don't let go until they get an answer.

When you have the Elijah anointing and you are being led by the unction of the Holy Spirit, you have the power and authority to pray effective, fervent prayers that avail much. You have the anointing to contend for the will of God to manifest in the earth. You have the determination to keep on asking with a desperate cry out of your spirit. And after you ask Him, you begin to seek Him. You move to another level where you keep on seeking Him—seeking His face, seeking His will, seeking His presence, seeking His counsel. You diligently seek answers and strategies. Then you begin to knock, praying for the Lord to open the doors so you can fulfill your assignment and turn the hearts of people back to the Lord.

Chapter 8

Miracles of Reformation

*E*LIJAH'S MINISTRY WAS marked by miracles. They were part of his calling, part of his assignment. They were physical manifestations of the message he had been given. The miracles God performed through Elijah were demonstrations of God at work to revive, reform, and restore His people and draw them back to Him. Each miracle provides a landmark or road sign to help us identify God's intentions and His heart for His people.

The miracles of reformation the Lord worked through Elijah demonstrated His righteous anger at the things that come to steal the hearts of His people away from Him. These miracles show God's commitment to protecting and defending His people against evil influences and demonic infiltration. While destruction can sometimes feel negative and we may grieve what it seems like we are losing, God's destruction of the things that separate us from Him demonstrates His overwhelming love for us. He fights for us. He will do the miraculous to try to get our attention and turn our hearts back to Him.

Reformation

Reformation is the act of being reformed. *Reform* means "to put or change into an improved form or condition; to amend or improve by change of form or removal of faults or abuses; to put an end to (an evil) by enforcing or introducing a better method or course of action; to induce or cause to abandon evil ways...to become changed for the better."[1] When the children of God have fallen into evil ways, they need to be reformed. They need to repent, to turn completely away from their wickedness and back toward the Lord. They need to put an end to their sin and idolatry and choose righteousness, holiness, and life.

The Greek word for *reformation* means to straighten thoroughly.[2] The Hebrew word for *reform* is *yāsar*. It means to discipline, to teach, to instruct, to chasten, to chastise, to punish, to correct, to reform, or to admonish.[3] It is used in passages such as:

> And if by these things you are not *reformed* by Me, but walk contrary to Me, then I also will walk contrary to you.
> —LEVITICUS 26:23–24, EMPHASIS ADDED

> Out of heaven He let you hear His voice, that He might *instruct* you; on earth He showed you His great fire, and you heard His words out of the midst of the fire.
> —DEUTERONOMY 4:36, EMPHASIS ADDED

> You should know in your heart that as a man *chastens* his son, so the LORD your God *chastens* you.
> —DEUTERONOMY 8:5, EMPHASIS ADDED

The present-day church finds itself in critical need of reformation, much like Israel did during the days of the prophet Elijah. Just as reformation was necessary for Israel to prepare the way for God's glory to be revealed, the church also requires a renewal and transformation to pave the path for the manifestation of God's glory.

In the days of Elijah, Israel had drifted away from God's commands, embracing idolatry and immorality, which led to spiritual decay and a departure from the true worship of the Almighty. Similarly, the contemporary church faces challenges such as complacency, division, and compromising with the world's values, diluting the purity of its faith and message.

Reformation in the church seeks to bring about a return to the foundational truths of the gospel, a revival of genuine faith, and a restoration of the core teachings of Christ. It involves a deep examination of doctrines, practices, and attitudes, with a commitment to realigning with God's Word and His heart.

Just as Elijah's prophetic ministry called for a turning of hearts back to the one true God, today's call for reformation urges believers to repent and seek a renewed relationship with God. Through genuine repentance and revival, the church can once again experience the power and presence of the Holy Spirit, leading to transformational growth and spiritual awakening.

Reformation is not merely about correcting errors or addressing surface-level issues; it is a profound process of seeking God's face, humbling oneself before Him, and surrendering to His will. It requires a willingness to let go of human traditions and preferences that have strayed from biblical truths and embracing God's ways.

The purpose of reformation in the church is to prepare the way for the glory of God to be fully manifested in the lives of believers and the church as a whole. It involves a restoration of spiritual fervor, passion for righteousness, and a deep commitment to holiness. When the church undergoes reformation and returns to its first love for Christ, it sets the stage for God's glory to be revealed, transforming lives, communities, and even nations with the power of His presence.

Matthew 9:16–17 says, "No one puts a piece of unshrunk cloth on an old garment; for the patch pulls away from the garment, and the tear is made worse. Nor do they put new wine into old wineskins, or else the wineskins break, the wine is spilled, and the wineskins are ruined. But they put new wine into new wineskins, and both are preserved." We can't be afraid of change. We can't be so entrenched in the traditions of man that we stop hearing from the Lord. We can't place fitting in with the world and adhering to society's standards above following the Word of God and preaching the truth of the gospel to a lost and dying world. The church needs to reform, to change. The change is necessary, but the change can't be superficial. Reformation is about starting afresh, being made new. We don't just need to put a bandage on it. We don't need to be conformed to the world; we need to be transformed by the renewing of our minds. We need the God of all things to make "all things new" (Rev. 21:5).

We are in a season when we can't put an unshrunk piece of cloth on an old garment because the rip will be made even worse. We need to embrace change, embrace reformation. That is why Elijah was so adamant and so direct with the people of Israel. They had built so many altars to false gods and turned away from the true and living God. They had succumbed to the pressure of the culture around them and fallen far. Because of that, they couldn't just put a little patch on things. They had to repent, tear down the false altars, and completely rebuild the altar of the Lord. They had to be reformed.

The church culture has allowed worldliness to creep in, and we have embraced secularism. It's like when cancer invades the human body and begins to replicate, moving through the bloodstream from organ to organ and eventually spreading throughout the entire body. If you catch the cancer early and deal with it, removing all the cancer cells, the cancer won't spread because all the malignancy is gone. But once it has spread to other parts of the body, you can't just remove the cancer from the place where it started—you need to get rid of all of it. Your entire body needs to be healed, transformed, refreshed, renewed, and made whole.

The church is the body of Christ. Colossians 1:18 says, "And [Jesus Christ] is the head of the body, the church, who is the beginning, the firstborn from the dead, that in all things He may have the preeminence." Romans 12:5 says, "So we, being many, are one body in Christ, and individually members of one another."

As the body of Christ, I believe we need to change the form—the structure, the system—of how we do church. This is not the time to try to patch an old garment or put new wine into old wineskins. We need to address the issues at their root. We cannot simply patch up the existing system or try to integrate worldly ideologies into our faith. Instead, we must repent of allowing worldliness, political correctness, secularism, and tolerance to infiltrate and spread within the church like a cancer. We must dismantle the false altars built to appease others and reconstruct the foundation of genuine worship to the one true God.

To reform the church, we must return to authentic worship, offering praise and adoration to God in spirit and truth. We need to fearlessly teach the whole counsel of the Word of God, unapologetically declaring the powerful name of Jesus as the only path to salvation. We should abandon fear or embarrassment in proclaiming the truth and boldly declare that Jesus Christ is the only One who can redeem, reform, and restore. In doing so, we will regain our purpose as the body of Christ, with Jesus as our head, and live in accordance with His preeminence.

The Purpose of Miracles

The Lord performed miracles of reformation through Elijah, and their purpose was not to condemn people but rather to have them turn back to the Lord. They were miracles of judgment on demonic systems.

Another purpose of miracles is to restore the awe of the Lord back into the hearts of men. Just as Israel had gotten too familiar with God in the days of Elijah, we also have gotten too familiar with God. That familiarity often allows people to easily dismiss the Lord or discount His power. When God releases miracles, it makes us wonder. It stirs up awe for the Lord God Almighty, Maker of heaven and earth. It causes us to tremble at His Word. It moves us once again to be people who will stand in wonder and bow down and worship Him in spirit and truth.

God is granting access to the realm of miracles. They shall stand as undeniable signs of the presence of the Almighty, showcasing His divine ability to intercede in the laws of nature. As the people bear witness to these wondrous events, their faith shall be fortified and a profound reverence and awe for God shall be kindled within their hearts.

We are in a season when we need the Elijah prophets to press into and preach miracles. We need Elijahs to believe God for the miraculous, because every miracle has a message. Every miracle has a mantle. Every miracle is causing us to move forward and draw closer to the Lord.

Behind every miracle is the dunamis power of the Holy Ghost. The Holy Ghost doesn't release His miraculous dunamis power so we can build bigger ministries, have more social media followers, or gain earthly fame for ourselves. The Holy Ghost releases His dunamis power to turn hearts back to the Father. He longs to heal this nation. He longs to see His people turn back to Him. He longs to have all His children in right relationship with Him.

Dunamis (also rendered *dynamis*) is a Greek word that is most often translated as "power"[4]:

Then Jesus returned in the power of the Spirit to Galilee, and news of Him went out through all the surrounding region.

—LUKE 4:14

Now it happened on a certain day, as He was teaching, that there were Pharisees and teachers of the law sitting by, who had come out of every town of Galilee, Judea, and Jerusalem. And the power of the Lord was present to heal them.

—LUKE 5:17

Then He called His twelve disciples together and gave them power and authority over all demons, and to cure diseases.

—LUKE 9:1

But you shall receive power when the Holy Spirit has come upon you; and you shall be witnesses to Me in Jerusalem, and in all Judea and Samaria, and to the end of the earth.

—ACTS 1:8

And Stephen, full of faith and power, did great wonders and signs among the people.

—ACTS 6:8

Dunamis also means mighty works, or force.[5] When you are walking in the spirit and power of Elijah, you have the dunamis of the Holy Ghost in you. So when you speak the Word, when you preach repentance and righteousness, when you bring words of correction and reformation, a Holy Ghost force will be on your words. Job 6:25 says, "How forceful are right words!" As Elijah prophets, when we get in the presence of God and listen for the right words, those words are going to carry the miraculous force of the Holy Ghost's dunamis power when we speak them. And not only that, but the Holy Spirit will watch over those words to perform them.

Dunamis also means might.[6] The prophet Isaiah wrote of the sevenfold Spirits, the seven flows of the Holy Spirit: "The Spirit of the LORD shall rest upon Him, the Spirit of wisdom and understanding, the Spirit of counsel and might, the Spirit of knowledge and of the fear of the LORD" (Isa. 11:2). As Elijah prophets, we need every aspect of the Spirit of the Lord, but when it comes to calling forth the miraculous, we need the Spirit of might. When you are carrying the spirit and power of Elijah, God will cause the anointing of might to come upon you, and you will do things you have never dreamed of or imagined. The Spirit of might is an impetus. It has the ability to catapult you. The Spirit of might gives you the ability to work miracles of reformation at the direction of the Lord.

Dunamis also means strength.[7] A mighty strength is coming for the Elijah prophets in this hour, and that strength comes with the anointing of the Lord—the dunamis anointing. The prophets will be filled with the knowledge of His will in all wisdom and spiritual understanding. Elijah prophets need to be strengthened in their hearts and minds. Because of the attacks the enemy will bring against them, they need the dunamis strength of the Holy Ghost to defend them. They need the miraculous dunamis of the Spirit to not give in to rejection, the fear of man, self-pity, or one of the other pitfalls Elijahs are prone to. The Scripture speaks of "men's hearts failing them from fear" (Luke 21:26). But I decree and declare that the strength of God will come upon all those called to be Elijah prophets in this season, and that they will be strong in the Lord and in the power of His might.

Dunamis also carries the meaning of ability and miraculous power.[8] Miraculous power is available from the Spirit of the Lord, and it is time for Elijahs to rise up and put a demand on that power, to put a demand on miracles.

MIRACLE OF DROUGHT

The first miracle of reformation was the miracle of drought. Drought is the withholding of rain. In an agricultural society, rain is everything—without it, crops dry up, there is nothing to harvest, and the people don't have food to eat or crops to sell to purchase other necessities. When the rain comes, the harvest comes. When the rain comes, a refreshing comes. Rain signifies fruitfulness and abundance. Rain is a symbol of blessing, especially financial blessing in an agrarian culture. So when the Lord withholds the rain, it symbolizes the withholding of His blessing.

One of the false gods that Israel was worshipping instead of the Lord was Baal. Among other things, Baal was believed by the Canaanites to be the god of rain and dew, the god of the sky and the elements. He was the one the pagans would pray to or sacrifice to for there to be the right amount of rain for their crops to grow and flourish. So when Elijah told Ahab, "As the LORD God of Israel lives, before whom I stand, there shall not be dew nor rain these years, except at my word" (1 Kings 17:1), it was an intentional, direct attack on Baal.

Baal was also the god of wealth and prosperity. His name actually means lord or owner.[9] So again, withholding the rain—and withholding financial blessing by doing so—was a direct attack on the lies of a false god.

Over the next three years, no matter what people did to try to get Baal to make it rain, there was no rain. Keep in mind that Israel was the Promised Land, the land of milk and honey. When Moses first sent spies into the Promised Land, they came back with just one cluster of grapes so big it had to be carried on a pole between two men. Drought was clearly not a problem they typically faced. So when the drought began and then continued for over three years, God was demonstrating that it was not Baal who controlled the rain and dew; it was not Baal who was the source of wealth and financial blessing—it was the Lord.

God revealed Himself as the supreme power over every realm—the atmosphere, the heavens, the earth, under the earth. The psalms speak of His power over creation and everything in it:

> Let them praise the name of the LORD, for He commanded and they were created. He also established them forever and ever; He made a decree which shall not pass away. Praise the LORD from the earth, you great sea creatures and all the depths; fire and hail, snow and clouds; stormy wind, fulfilling His word; mountains and all hills; fruitful trees and all cedars; beasts and all cattle; creeping things and flying fowl; kings of the earth and all peoples; princes and all judges of the earth; both young men and maidens; old men and children.
>
> —PSALM 148:5–12

God created the earth and everything in it, and even the stormy wind and weather is fulfilling His Word. When God speaks and says there won't be rain, Baal—or any other false god or demonic entity—is powerless to make it rain. And when God says it's going to rain, Baal is powerless to stop it.

With the miracle of the drought, God was revealing His greatness to a people who had forgotten just how great He is. They had forgotten His goodness, His mercy, and His grace. The drought was a wake-up call to the people about the true source of their blessings. The Lord was also vindicating Himself, His Word, and His sovereignty, as well as His anointing on the prophets.

The drought was a miracle that initiated reformation. It was a judgment on the children of Israel for their idolatry, but it was also the cry of a loving God to His people: "Turn back!

Come home! Don't fall for the lies of the enemy! I am the true source of all that you need!"

When Elijah declared that drought, he was still living in the land and would have to continue to do so to fulfill the calling on his life. But even in the face of a drought, God sustained him. Elijah never went hungry; he never went thirsty. God met his every need. God first provided for Elijah at the Brook Cherith, and He later used the widow of Zarephath. Both the brook and the widow were part of God's plan for Elijah.

When you are walking in the spirit and power of Elijah, the Lord may call you to declare a drought in the land, whether physical or spiritual. But just because you declare the drought does not mean you are going to dry up. God is going to do certain things in your life for which no one else will be able to get the glory. The Lord will reveal Himself as the sustainer of your life—no matter what circumstances occur.

MIRACLE OF FIRE

The second miracle of reformation was the miracle of fire. The showdown on Mount Carmel centered on "the God who answers by fire" (1 Kings 18:24). No matter what the prophets of Baal did that day on the mountain, there was no response from their false god. They cried out, leaped around, and even cut themselves, but there was only silence.

When Elijah's turn came it was a different story. He orchestrated the circumstances to make sure that no one other than the Lord could get credit for the fire that was about to fall. He soaked the altar and the sacrifice from top to bottom. Yet when the moment came, when he called upon the Lord to send fire so the people would know the Lord was God and turn their hearts back to Him, "the fire of the Lord fell and consumed the burnt sacrifice, and the wood and the stones and the dust, and it licked up the water that was in the trench" (1 Kings 18:38).

The fire of the Lord represents many things. There is the fire of the Holy Ghost, as when the tongues of fire appeared above the disciples in the Upper Room (Acts 2:3). The Lord went before the children of Israel through the wilderness for forty years with a pillar of fire by night (Exod. 13:21). When Moses met with the Lord on top of Mount Sinai, "the LORD descended upon [the mountain] in fire," and "the sight of the glory of the LORD was like a consuming fire on the top of the mountain in the eyes of the children of Israel" (Exod. 19:18; 24:17). The Lord talked to Moses "face to face on the mountain from the midst of the fire" (Deut. 5:4). God's Word is like fire (Jer. 23:29). In both the tabernacle and the temple, offerings were made by fire to the Lord. Psalm 104:4 says the Lord "makes His angels spirits, His ministers a flame of fire."

Fire also purifies and refines. When Isaiah was called to be a prophet and saw the Lord sitting on His throne, he cried, "Woe is me, for I am undone! Because I am a man of unclean lips, and I dwell in the midst of a people of unclean lips; for my eyes have seen the King, the LORD of hosts." Then an angel took a live coal from the altar and touched Isaiah's mouth with it and said, "Behold, this has touched your lips; your iniquity is taken away, and your sin purged" (Isa. 6:5, 7). The Scripture also says:

> For He is like a refiner's fire and like launderers' soap. He will sit as a refiner and a purifier of silver; He will purify the sons of Levi, and purge them as gold and silver, that they may offer to the LORD an offering in righteousness.
>
> —MALACHI 3:2–3

Fire is often an act or a symbol of judgment too. God "rained brimstone and fire on Sodom and Gomorrah" (Gen. 19:24).

When the children of Israel were constantly complaining, "it displeased the LORD; for the LORD heard it, and His anger was aroused. So the fire of the LORD burned among them, and consumed some in the outskirts of the camp" (Num. 11:1). The Lord told Jeremiah, "I will make My words in your mouth fire, and this people wood, and it shall devour them" (Jer. 5:14). And when Nadab and Abihu, Aaron's sons and priests of the Lord, offered strange fire before the Lord, "fire went out from the LORD and devoured them, and they died before the LORD" (Lev. 10:2).

In this context, *strange fire* refers to an unauthorized or improper offering presented to God. In a broader spiritual sense, *strange fire* refers to practices, beliefs, or actions that are considered unacceptable or contrary to the true principles of a particular faith or religious tradition. It can signify unauthorized worship, false teachings, or anything that deviates from the genuine and prescribed way of connecting with the divine.

The prophetic calling of Elijah—an anointing that confronts and dismantles false prophets and strange fire—shall be ignited once again within the body of Christ. In this present time, there will be a surge of deceptive practices and misguided teachings that seek to lead God's people astray. But fear not, for those anointed with the spirit of Elijah shall rise with boldness and conviction. They will confront falsehoods, uphold divine truth, and restore the purity of worship and service. Through their unwavering dedication, the authenticity of the faith shall be preserved, and the true light of God's Word will shine brightly, guiding the church toward righteousness and obedience. Embrace the Elijah anointing, for it heralds a season of purification and spiritual awakening within the body of Christ.

Elijah prophets must warn against adopting practices that are not in alignment with the core teachings and values of the faith. The warning serves as a cautionary reminder to stay true to the authentic path and avoid engaging in misguided or deceptive practices in matters of spirituality and worship.

When the fire fell on Mount Carmel, it was first an act of judgment against the idolatry and wickedness of the children of Israel. But the fire was also an act of purification, of refining. It came to purify the altar of the Lord. It came to burn away the things that had gotten between the Lord and His people. It came to consume all that was not of the Lord so they could rebuild from scratch and be both reformed and transformed.

The fire that fell was also an act of empowerment. When God answered by fire, it was a sign of the reestablishment of His presence in the hearts of His people. It was an unquestionable sign of His power at work to rescue His children from their own foolishness.

Before the fire came, before the miracles came, the Lord used Elijah to challenge Israel's allegiance. And then, when Elijah built that altar of worship, the fire fell. It wasn't from a place of revenge, for God does not have a spirit of revenge. He was trying to get His people to turn back to Him. He sent the fire so the spirit of conviction could come. Jesus said, "Unless you people see signs and wonders, you will by no means believe" (John 4:48). Some people won't believe unless they see a sign. Because the Lord knows that, He sent a sign to Israel to turn their hearts back to Him.

Elijah's message was clear: if the Lord is God, follow Him! The Lord sent a miracle to validate the message. He validated His messenger as well. When you choose the ways of God and recognize that it's more important to be righteous than to be right, God will validate you and the message He has given you. The way of the righteous is not easy, but it is possible. And when you choose the Lord, He will answer with fire.

Chapter 9

The Forerunner

JOHN THE BAPTIST was the forerunner of Jesus, the Messiah coming to save the world. A forerunner is "one that precedes and indicates the approach of another."[1] The word occurs just once in the Bible, in reference to Jesus: "This hope we have as an anchor of the soul, both sure and steadfast, and which enters the Presence behind the veil, where the forerunner has entered for us, even Jesus, having become High Priest forever according to the order of Melchizedek" (Heb. 6:19–20). The Greek word for *forerunner* refers to someone who runs ahead to scout a location or goes in advance to a place where others will follow.[2]

While the word *forerunner* may only be used once in the Bible, the concept is there in many places. A forerunner is someone who goes ahead to prepare the way, and that is exactly what John the Baptist did for Jesus at His first coming. I believe the Lord is raising up Elijah prophets in this hour to be the forerunners of Jesus' second coming. The Word of God describes what the world will be like in the last days before Jesus returns:

> But know this, that in the last days perilous times will come: For men will be lovers of themselves, lovers of money, boasters, proud, blasphemers, disobedient to parents, unthankful, unholy, unloving, unforgiving, slanderers, without self-control, brutal, despisers of good, traitors, headstrong, haughty, lovers of pleasure rather than lovers of God, having a form of godliness but denying its power. And from such people turn away! For of this sort are those who creep into households and make captives of gullible women loaded down with sins, led away by various lusts, always learning and never able to come to the knowledge of the truth.
>
> —2 TIMOTHY 3:1–7

There is no doubt that Paul's words to Timothy describe the world we are living in today. We are in the last days, so we need Elijah prophets to prepare the way. God is raising up modern-day forerunners, individuals uniquely chosen and anointed to fulfill a vital role. Their mission is to prepare the way for the imminent visitation of the Lord.

As trailblazers and pioneers, these forerunners will go ahead, clearing the path for the divine presence to manifest in power and glory. Through their dedicated ministry, they will call the hearts of people to repentance, revival, and a deeper intimacy with God. They will ignite a passion for righteousness and usher in a season of spiritual awakening.

THE COMING OF JOHN THE BAPTIST

The angel who appeared to Zacharias gave a clear prophecy about John the Baptist's assignment:

> For he will be great in the sight of the Lord, and shall
> drink neither wine nor strong drink. He will also be
> filled with the Holy Spirit, even from his mother's womb.
> And he will turn many of the children of Israel to the
> Lord their God. He will also go before Him in the spirit
> and power of Elijah, "to turn the hearts of the fathers
> to the children," and the disobedient to the wisdom of
> the just, to make ready a people prepared for the Lord.
> —LUKE 1:15–17

The spiritual markers to identify modern-day Elijah prophets can also be found in the words of Luke 1:15–17.

"Great in the sight of the Lord"—These prophets
will have a significant spiritual impact and be
highly esteemed by God for their dedication and
obedience. They will not look for the approval of
men.

"Abstain from worldly indulgences"—They will lead
lives of self-discipline and consecration, refraining
from practices that may hinder their spiritual
sensitivity.

"Filled with the Holy Spirit"—These prophets will be
deeply immersed in the Holy Spirit, carrying a
powerful anointing from an early age.

"Turn many to the Lord"—Through their ministry,
they will bring about repentance and lead others
to a genuine relationship with God.

"Spirit and power of Elijah"—These prophets will
walk in the anointing and authority of Elijah,
mirroring his boldness, courage, and fervent
dedication to God.

"Reconciling families"—They will have a heart to heal
broken relationships and restore harmony within
families and communities.

"Bring wisdom to the disobedient"—Through divine
insight, they will impart God's wisdom to those
who have strayed from His ways.

"Preparing people for the Lord"—These prophets will
serve as instruments in readying the hearts of
people for the coming of the Lord, preparing
them to receive Him with open and repentant
hearts.

By observing these spiritual markers, we can discern the
authentic Elijah prophets in our midst, who are being raised
up by God to carry out His divine purposes and usher in His
kingdom on earth.

John the Baptist was prophesied to come in the spirit and
power of Elijah. He was going to be filled with the Holy
Spirit, even in his mother's womb—which was fulfilled when
he leaped inside Elizabeth's womb when Mary, pregnant with
Jesus, entered the house (Luke 1:41). Just as Elijah did, he
turned the hearts of many of the children of Israel back to the
Lord. And as Malachi prophesied, he turned "the hearts of the
fathers to the children" (Mal. 4:6). It was all to "make ready a
people prepared for the Lord" (Luke 1:17).

When Jewish boys were born, their names were not publicly
announced until they were circumcised at eight days old.
When the time came to name John, the people assumed he
would be called Zacharias, like his father. But both Elizabeth
and Zacharias said his name would be John, just as the angel
Gabriel told Zacharias. The name John means "the Lord is a
gracious giver."[3] It was a fitting name for John, both because
he was a gift to his parents, who had long been childless, and
because he would prepare the way for the One who was the
greatest, most gracious gift the world has ever known—Jesus.

After John was named, his father, Zacharias, was filled
with the Holy Spirit and prophesied about Jesus redeeming

and saving His people in fulfillment of God's covenant with Abraham. He also prophesied about John, saying:

> And you, child, will be called the prophet of the Highest; for you will go before the face of the Lord to prepare His ways, to give knowledge of salvation to His people by the remission of their sins, through the tender mercy of our God, with which the Dayspring from on high has visited us; to give light to those who sit in darkness and the shadow of death, to guide our feet into the way of peace.
>
> —LUKE 1:76–79

Those verses are a description of the calling and purpose of the child who would become known as the prophet of the Highest. Here are the key spiritual markers of this prophet's mission:

Forerunner of the Lord—This prophet would go before the Lord to pave the way and prepare people for His coming.

Bearer of salvation—His ministry would bring knowledge of salvation and the forgiveness of sins to God's people.

Instrument of God's mercy—The prophet's work would be driven by the tender mercy of our God, extending grace and compassion to those in need.

Bearer of the Dayspring—This prophet would carry the message of the Dayspring from on high, representing the coming of a new dawn and hope for humanity.

Bringer of light—The prophet's calling would be to shine a light on those who dwell in darkness and the shadow of death, offering hope and illumination.

Guide to peace—The prophet's mission would lead people on a path of peace and reconciliation with God.

In these verses we see a prophetic foreshadowing of the work that John the Baptist would undertake as the forerunner of Jesus Christ, preparing the way for the Savior's ministry of salvation and offering the gift of peace to all who believe. It's a powerful testament to God's plan of redemption for humanity and the role of prophets in fulfilling His divine purposes.

But John needed to be prepared for his role. So the very next verse after Zacharias' prophecy says, "So the child grew and became strong in spirit, and was in the deserts till the day of his manifestation to Israel" (Luke 1:80). That was the beginning of John's wilderness time, a time that lasted until he was thirty years old and began his ministry.

As I said before, the wilderness time is critically important for Elijah prophets. They need the time hidden away with the Lord to be refined, refreshed, and renewed. They need to be washed by the water of the Word. They need to spend time in close communion with the Holy Spirit, learning to hear His voice.

John the Baptist spent three decades in the wilderness. There are no shortcuts through the wilderness season. It will last as long as the Lord thinks you need. It is a time of waiting, which can make people impatient, but if you are wise you will take advantage of that waiting season to grow closer and closer to the Lord and become more and more like Jesus. The preparation that occurs in the wilderness will help you to fulfill your assignment and stay in the will of God even when troubles come and the enemy attacks.

John the Baptist's message was straightforward: "Repent!" He didn't need fancy words and catchy sermon illustrations and engaging PowerPoint slides. He just preached the truth—and it was very effective. Everyone was heading out to the wilderness to hear him preach: "Then Jerusalem, all Judea, and all the region around the Jordan went out to him" (Matt. 3:5). And while I am sure some people went out to the wilderness to be entertained or, in the case of the Pharisees and Sadducees, to criticize, John the Baptist did indeed begin to turn hearts back to the Lord. People were "baptized by him in the Jordan, confessing their sins" (Matt. 3:6).

John called the children of Israel to repent, just as Elijah did. He also let them know that repentance wasn't just a one-time thing. They needed to walk in righteousness. They needed to be reformed. He told them, "Bear fruits worthy of repentance....Every tree which does not bear good fruit is cut down and thrown into the fire" (Matt. 3:8, 10).

This was a warning of the fire of judgment. John was particularly addressing the Pharisees and Sadducees, the religious rulers of the day who were more concerned about following religious rituals and traditions than following the Lord with pure hearts and pure hands. For most of them, their so-called faith was just a show, a theatrical production meant to make people think they were holy and righteous. The reality was that they were "like whitewashed tombs which indeed appear beautiful outwardly, but inside are full of dead men's bones and all uncleanness" (Matt. 23:27).

The call to righteousness is a key component of the Elijah anointing. Elijah called people to walk in righteousness before the Lord. John the Baptist did too. And the Elijahs of today also have the assignment to call people to righteousness, to live according to the Word of God, to be holy and set apart for the Lord.

John the Baptist also prophesied about another fire—the fire of the Holy Spirit. But in the same prophecy, he also warned again about the fire of judgment:

> I indeed baptize you with water unto repentance, but He who is coming after me is mightier than I, whose sandals I am not worthy to carry. He will baptize you with the Holy Spirit and fire. His winnowing fan is in His hand, and He will thoroughly clean out His threshing

floor, and gather His wheat into the barn; but He will
burn up the chaff with unquenchable fire.

—MATTHEW 3:11–12

This is the dual nature of the fire of the Lord. On one hand
we have the fire of the Spirit and all the benefits it brings. But
on the other hand we have the fire of judgment that comes to
purge and burn away anything that is not of the Lord. Elijah
prophets bring both kinds of fire.

PREPARE THE WAY

Isaiah prophesied about John the Baptist as the forerunner of
Jesus hundreds of years before his birth:

"Comfort, yes, comfort My people!" says your God.
"Speak comfort to Jerusalem, and cry out to her, that
her warfare is ended, that her iniquity is pardoned; for
she has received from the LORD's hand double for all
her sins." The voice of one crying in the wilderness:
"Prepare the way of the LORD; make straight in the desert
a highway for our God. Every valley shall be exalted and
every mountain and hill brought low; the crooked places
shall be made straight and the rough places smooth; the
glory of the LORD shall be revealed, and all flesh shall
see it together; for the mouth of the LORD has spoken."

—ISAIAH 40:1–7

As forerunners of the Messiah, those who walk in the spirit
and power of Elijah, like John the Baptist, are preparing the
way for the Lord. They will be a voice crying out from the
wilderness, not an echo. The voice will be controversial, but
the cry will compel men to stop and listen. They make the
crooked places straight and the rough places smooth.

The Hebrew word for *crooked* doesn't just mean bent or
not straight; it also means fraudulent, deceitful, insidious,

sly, or polluted.[4] The Hebrew word for *rough* means bound up, impassable, impeded, hard, and calamitous.[5] This is the setting for Elijahs.

The original Elijah was called to a society that had turned away from the Lord and turned to idols. Their hearts were hard, impeded by the callousness resulting from their sin. Their culture had been polluted by idolatry, witchcraft, sexual licentiousness, child sacrifice, and many other forms of wickedness.

John the Baptist was called to a society that had also turned away from the Lord. After four hundred years of silence, many may have either forgotten the Lord or thought He had forgotten them. The role of high priest in the temple of the Lord had become a political position to be bought and sold rather than the position of a righteous spiritual leader of a nation. The temple of the Lord was polluted by the deceptive practices of the moneychangers and the vendors selling animals for sacrifice, not to mention some of the priests themselves.

The Elijahs of today are living in a society that has turned away from the Lord. Our culture is permeated by deception and fraud. The church has been polluted by tolerance and political correctness and the watering down of the Word of God. People's hearts have been hardened to sin to the point that they don't even recognize that they are bound up in chains because of it.

But while Elijahs come to places that are both crooked and rough, they come to make them straight and smooth. That is where the call to repent and the call to righteousness come in. The Hebrew word for *straight* means level, straight, upright, right, righteous, and justice.[6] The word translated "smooth" refers to a plain, a level valley, or a split.[7]

Those who walk in the spirit and power of Elijah come with a call to live righteously, to walk the straight and narrow path, to be upright in one's words and actions. They come to smooth out all the rough places caused by our sin and to cause a split between the old way of doing things and the new way. Elijah prophets carve out a highway of holiness for God's people.

Elijah prophets do not mince words or cower to the intimidation of powerful people. Elijah was blunt and bold when he faced Ahab, Jezebel, and the prophets of Baal. John the Baptist was blunt and bold when he faced Herod, Herodias, and the Pharisees and Sadducees. And the Elijahs of today must be blunt and bold when they face people in authority or religious leaders mired in tradition, wickedness, or anything else that is not of the Lord.

The assignment and calling of Elijah prophets is one of preparation. Their assignment is to prepare the way for the Lord by turning hearts back to Him. It is also to prepare the way for the glory of the Lord. There is a promise in Isaiah's prophecy: "the glory of the LORD shall be revealed" (Isa. 40:5).

Elijah prepared the way, and the glory of the Lord was revealed when fire fell from heaven, as well as when his other miracles occurred. John the Baptist prepared the way, and the glory of the Lord was revealed in the person of Jesus Christ, the Messiah, the Lamb of God who came to take away the sins of the world:

> And the Word became flesh and dwelt among us, and we beheld His glory, the glory as of the only begotten of the Father, full of grace and truth.
>
> —JOHN 1:14

And after the Elijahs of this season—this time in history—prepare the way, the glory of the Lord will be revealed not only in the miracles that occur but also when Jesus comes back again:

> The glory of the LORD shall be revealed, and all flesh shall see it together; for the mouth of the LORD has spoken.
>
> —ISAIAH 40:5

The forerunners of this age are diligently preparing the way for the most magnificent display and revelation of God's glory. When His glory manifests, it will be a sight witnessed by all, without exception. Critics will be rendered speechless, skeptics will be left in awe, and agnostics will find faith in abundance. Even atheists will tremble in the presence of God's overwhelming power. Sinners will be gripped with fear, and the righteous will rejoice in His holy presence.

Backsliders will be moved to repentance, and the indifferent will be shaken from their complacency. The spiritually fervent will be set ablaze with passion, while those who were spiritually cold will be compelled to make a life-altering decision. Both the young and the elderly will experience a revitalizing touch, and the hardened hearts will face divine judgment. The harvest of souls will be gathered, and the heavenly Father will be glorified in this momentous revelation.

During this unparalleled time, humanity will collectively witness undeniable manifestations of God's reality. All will be compelled to confess, "Truly, God is among them!" I am describing the indescribable and glorious reality that awaits us! For we are the demonstration generation.

THE HAND OF THE LORD

Another characteristic of the spirit and power of Elijah is the hand of the Lord. The phrase *hand of the Lord* or *the Lord's hand* is in the Bible forty-two times. Sometimes the hand of the Lord is moving in judgment, as in Deuteronomy 2:15: "For indeed the hand of the LORD was against them, to destroy them." Sometimes the hand of the Lord brings favor, as it did for Ezra before the king of Persia (Ezra 7:6). And sometimes the hand of the Lord is the supernatural empowerment of the Holy Spirit.

After the showdown on Mount Carmel, Elijah sent Ahab up

the mountain to eat and drink. But once his servant confirmed that the rain was coming, he told his servant, "Go up, say to Ahab, 'Prepare your chariot, and go down before the rain stops you'" (1 Kings 18:44). Ahab once again followed Elijah's instructions, and he rode his chariot back to Jezreel in the midst of clouds, wind, and heavy rain.

Then there was another miracle: "The hand of the LORD came upon Elijah; and he girded up his loins and ran ahead of Ahab to the entrance of Jezreel" (1 Kings 18:46). The distance from Mount Carmel to Jezreel was about fifteen miles. For some people, running that distance at all would be a miracle, but Elijah not only ran the whole way, he arrived in Jezreel ahead of Ahab.

Elijah was on assignment, and with all that had happened that day, he knew he needed to be in Jezreel. He was in tune with the Lord, and so he knew that his presence in Jezreel as the voice of repentance, the voice of reformation, and the voice of return was vital—for whenever God moves in such a miraculous way, the devil will do everything in his power to make people doubt, disbelieve, and turn away from the Lord again. And that is exactly what happened.

Ahab, who had started to listen to Elijah and heed the word of the Lord, went home and told his wife, Jezebel, what had happened. Jezebel's heart wasn't moved to repent. She didn't fall on her face in recognition that the Lord is God. She was so bound up in idolatry and witchcraft that when she heard about Elijah executing the prophets of Baal, she said, "So let the gods do to me, and more also, if I do not make your life as the life of one of them by tomorrow about this time" (1 Kings 19:2).

The hand of the Lord gave Elijah supernatural strength. Remember that chariots represent man-made systems of power. But when the hand of the Lord is upon your life, you have the ability to overcome every man-made system or structure designed to stop you and prevent you from fulfilling your assignment. Ahab had a chariot and Elijah didn't, but that wasn't going to get in the way of what God wanted to accomplish. When the Creator of all things is involved, all things are possible. God isn't bound by natural laws because He is the One who invented them. He is supernatural, and there is nothing He can't do, no obstacle He can't move out of the way, and no man-made system that can stop Him from working His wonders. Psalm 20:7 says, "Some trust in chariots, and some in horses; but we will remember the name of the LORD our God." His name is mighty to save, and His hand is more powerful than anything the devil might try to bring against you.

> Your right hand, O LORD, has become glorious in power; Your right hand, O LORD, has dashed the enemy in pieces.
>
> —EXODUS 15:6

God is going to shut down whatever man-made system has been set up against you. You don't have to pledge your allegiance to any person or man-made system. You just pledge your allegiance to God. Do you remember how Jesus, when talking about John the Baptist, likened His generation to children complaining about playing the flute and people not dancing to it (Matt. 11:16–17)? You have the hand of the Lord on you, so you don't have to dance or play the flute. You don't have to try to fit into somebody's club. You don't have to try to please people, looking for validation. You don't have to do things out of a spirit of performance. The Lord is breaking the spirit of performance because He validates you when He puts His hand on you.

Elijah was not the only prophet who experienced the hand of the Lord upon him. The hand of the Lord came upon Elisha (2 Kings 3:15) and Ezekiel (Ezek. 1:3). And the hand of the Lord was also on John the Baptist, for Luke 1:66 says, "And the hand of the Lord was with him."

When you are walking in the spirit and power of Elijah, the hand of the Lord will come upon you. It may give you supernatural empowerment to do something that would otherwise be physically impossible, just as Elijah did. But there are other signs of the hand of the Lord resting upon you; provision, protection, favor, signs, wonders, and miracles are just a few. In the case of Elijahs, you will also experience "the Spirit of wisdom and understanding, the Spirit of counsel and might, the Spirit of knowledge and of the fear of the LORD" (Isa.11:2), and with that will come new authority and power to destroy the enemies of your destiny.

Chapter 10

Who Is the Real Enemy?

FTER GREAT VICTORIES, Elijah prophets have to be very careful to guard and care for their souls, allowing God to restore them. The prophetic ministry frequently exposes prophets to intense and high-stakes situations, where the outcomes could lead to either success or failure, acceptance or rejection, vindication or humiliation, and even life or death. When prophets experience great success, witness victories, and bring about significant revival, they naturally expect appreciation and recognition from church leadership for their powerful prophetic words and actions. However, it is not uncommon for church leadership to respond how Queen Jezebel did—not with appreciation but with rejection and even threats of harm. As a result, prophets may become profoundly disheartened by such reactions.

Many times, in the aftermath of a great spiritual battle, prophets are more vulnerable because they are tired, exhausted even, and have expended all their physical and spiritual energy. The enemy knows this, and he will not hesitate to launch an immediate attack to try to silence the prophet in the future or even take them out of the picture completely be causing premature death. But in every battle, when you are walking in the spirit and power of Elijah, you must know who the real enemy is.

THE MESSENGER OF JEZEBEL

Imagine how Elijah must have felt. He had been called as a prophet to turn the hearts of the children of Israel back to the Lord. When he asked the people how long they would falter between two opinions and they didn't respond, I imagine the enemy tried to make him doubt, to make him fear that what he was doing in obedience to the Lord would have no effect in turning hearts.

But then the fire of the Lord fell.

Elijah must have been overwhelmed with joy and perhaps even relief at seeing the people fall on their faces before the Lord and declaring with all their hearts, "The LORD, He is God! The LORD, He is God!" (1 Kings 18:39). Executing the prophets of Baal must have brought a measure of relief too, knowing they would not be able to lead the Israelites astray again. And then Ahab—the king who had been trying to hunt him down and take him out for years—appeared to be having a change of heart. When Elijah told him to go up the mountain to eat and drink, Ahab obeyed. When Elijah told Ahab to go home to Jezreel, Ahab went home. Ahab wasn't arguing with Elijah or trying to kill him or condemning him or calling him the troubler of Israel anymore; he was doing whatever Elijah told him to do, even though he was a king and Elijah was one of his subjects.

On top of that, after a drought that lasted for over three years, Elijah prayed and the rain came. And it wasn't just a sprinkle or a light shower. An abundance of rain soaked the earth, blessing the people and the land, refreshing bodies and hearts, and washing away the past that had been polluting the land. Then the hand of the Lord came upon Elijah, and he was supernaturally empowered to run ahead of Ahab's chariot all the way to Jezreel. To see and experience the Lord doing all those things in the space of a day must have had Elijah on a spiritual high. He had been faithful to obey the unction of the Lord, to fulfill his assignment, to walk worthy of his calling, and God had responded faithfully and worked His amazing signs and wonders. What a day!

But Elijah also must have been weary. It had been a long road to that moment, and the day, while amazing, had to be physically, emotionally, and spiritually draining. And that is when the attack came.

> And Ahab told Jezebel all that Elijah had done, also how he had executed all the prophets with the sword. Then Jezebel sent a messenger to Elijah, saying, "So let the gods do to me, and more also, if I do not make your life as the life of one of them by tomorrow about this time."
> —1 KINGS 19:1–2

This was no empty threat. Jezebel's threat was real, and Elijah knew it. She killed the prophets of the Lord before, and she wouldn't hesitate to kill one more, especially one who had done what Elijah had done. Elijah knew who he was dealing with—a ruthless woman who hated the living God and His messengers. And in a clear demonstration that even prophets are all too human, Elijah ran for his life.

In the twenty-first century, the messenger of Jezebel may take on various forms, representing the spirit of manipulation, intimidation, and opposition to God's messengers. While not a literal person, the messenger of Jezebel symbolizes individuals or influences that seek to undermine and attack those who stand for God's truth and righteousness. Here are some ways the messenger of Jezebel may manifest in modern times:

Online trolls and cyberbullying—In the age of the internet and social media, the messenger of Jezebel may use deceitful tactics and threats to attack and harass individuals who speak out about their faith or advocate for biblical values.

False accusations and slander—The messenger of Jezebel seeks to tarnish the reputation of God's messengers, hoping to discredit them and hinder the impact of their ministry.

Opposition from worldly influences—The messenger of Jezebel may arise through influential figures, media, or organizations that actively oppose and denounce the biblical message.

Persecution and threats—Like Queen Jezebel's messenger threatening Elijah's life, the modern messenger of Jezebel may employ threats, intimidation, or even persecution to try and silence those who boldly proclaim God's truth.

Distorted teachings and false prophets—The messenger of Jezebel might propagate false teachings or follow false prophets who lead people away from the genuine faith and obedience to God.

Control and manipulation in church leadership—In certain church environments, the messenger of Jezebel could be represented by leaders who exercise authoritarian control and manipulate their followers, suppressing independent thought and genuine spiritual growth.

Spiritual compromise and syncretism—The messenger of Jezebel might advocate for a blending of Christianity with worldly ideologies or practices, leading believers away from pure devotion to God.

It is crucial for believers to be vigilant and recognize the influences of the messenger of Jezebel. By staying rooted in God's Word, seeking discernment through prayer, and remaining steadfast in their faith, God's messengers can navigate the challenges and opposition that may arise while continuing to shine the light of truth in a world that needs it more than ever.

JEZEBEL SPIRIT

Jezebel was the sworn enemy of Elijah because she was the sworn enemy of the Lord. Jezebel hated the one true God and all His prophets. Jezebel was a demonized woman filled with demons of witchcraft, idolatry, murder, and rebellion.

Jezebel was the daughter of Ethbaal, the king of Sidon. Ethbaal means "with Baal," or in other words, living under the favor of Baal.[1] So she was born into a Baal-worshipping society to a man who was fully entrenched in Baal worship and all its wicked and idolatrous practices.

Jezebel's name means "Baal exalts, Baal is husband to, unchaste, or unhusbanded."[2] Just her name shows that Jezebel was closely tied to Baal worship. However, the extent of her involvement went far beyond her name or even her personal worship of Baal. Jezebel was instrumental in leading Ahab to worship Baal, for it wasn't until after he married Jezebel that Ahab got serious about Baal worship:

> He took as wife Jezebel the daughter of Ethbaal, king of the Sidonians; and he went and served Baal and worshiped him. Then he set up an altar for Baal in the temple of Baal, which he had built in Samaria.
>
> —1 KINGS 16:31–32

Jezebel also supported the worship of both Baal and Asherah, another false god, by supporting their prophets. The Scripture tells us that 450 prophets of Baal and 400 prophets of Asherah dined at Jezebel's table (1 Kings 18:19). She was feeding 850 people every single day in support of the idolatry and wickedness of Israel. Even for a queen this was no small feat, especially during a drought that lasted for years. Jezebel clearly intended to remove the Lord from His rightful place as the God of Israel and put Baal there instead.

That is why Jezebel hated Elijah so much. Elijah had exposed the lie of Baal worship and revealed the glory and truth of the Lord God Almighty, and it made Jezebel furious. Elijah destroyed all her lies, seductions, manipulations, and power-hungry schemes, revealing that all she was living for, all she had centered her life around, was a lie.

The Jezebel spirit that wars against the Lord is still at work in the world today, and I believe Jezebel is especially at war with America. The Jezebel spirit still works to dethrone the Lord in the hearts of His people, to silence the word of the Lord, and to kill the prophets of the Lord.

Jezebel is a spirit of idolatry, witchcraft, seduction, and death. The spirit of Jezebel is seducing people with witchcraft, which is why witchcraft is on the rise in America. The spirit of Jezebel causes people to be in a state of demonic desperation, especially during times of drought or famine, whether natural or spiritual. That desperation makes people vulnerable to exploitation. The spirit of Jezebel causes people to die prematurely, especially the prophets of the Lord. The spirit of Jezebel tries to erect anything and everything in our hearts to take the place of God, leading us into idolatry.

The spirit of Jezebel moves in sexual seduction. Pornography is destroying marriages. In 2005, a marriage and family therapist testified before the US Senate that 56 percent of divorces involved a spouse having "an obsessive interest" in pornography—and that was almost twenty years ago; it is likely higher now. Pornography is leading men and women into all sorts of sexual deviance and perversion, increasing the risk of sexual deviancy and rape (as the perpetrator).[3] Pornography pushes people to continually succumb to the lusts of their flesh until they are in complete bondage to a pornography addiction. Jezebel is even going after our children with pornography. The average age children are first exposed to pornography is said to be between eleven and twelve years old, and viewing pornography as an adolescent is now considered "normal"—to the point where one study of US youth in late adolescence reported that over 80 percent of them had viewed pornography.[4]

The spirit of Jezebel is a baby killer. Remember that child sacrifice was part of idol worship during the days of Elijah. The spirit of abortion is rooted in Jezebel because it wants to kill the next generation. Jezebel's daughter, Athaliah, killed her own grandchildren to ensure that she stayed in power. Jezebel is behind the radical feminist movement that is killing our babies.

The spirit of Jezebel is also behind the war on gender distinction. God created us male and female—there is no other option, and you are what God created you to be. The devil is a liar, and his war on gender distinction through the spirit of Jezebel is an attack against true men of God, as is radical feminism. Remember, one of the meanings of Jezebel's name is "unhusbanded." If the spirit of Jezebel can get men to think they are women and women to think they don't need men, it emasculates true men of God. Jezebel wants to castrate men. The whole gender distinction battle and the lie that all masculinity is toxic is about men being destroyed, being removed from their God-given roles and assignments.

Jezebel is at war with America and the church. That is why the Elijah prophets need to rise up and say, "Not on my watch!" The prophets need to get away from Jezebel's table. Jezebel is a merchandising spirit, and too many prophets have been eating from her table. As prophets of the living God, we need to break and cancel every assignment of Jezebel that is coming against us—against our marriages, our families, our children, our churches, our identities, and our lives. We have to wake up and understand Jezebel's assignment against the church. The spirit of Jezebel comes to silence the prophets, so I decree, "Prophets, arise! Let your voices be heard!"

WHEN JEZEBEL THREATENS

When Jezebel threatened Elijah, he ran for his life. He went all the way to Beersheba in Judah, out of the kingdom ruled by Ahab and Jezebel.

While his initial reaction was to run away in fear, Elijah knew deep down what he really needed to do. He left his servant in Beersheba, "but he himself went a day's journey into the wilderness" (1 Kings 19:4). When he was overwhelmed by troubles and battling against the enemy of his soul, Elijah went to the wilderness.

While he was wise enough to obey the unction to hide himself away with the Lord once again, Elijah was still struggling. He was mired in a pit of doubt and self-pity. When he got to the wilderness, "he prayed that he might die, and said, 'It is enough! Now, LORD, take my life, for I am no better than my fathers!'" (1 Kings 19:4). If Elijah had died sitting under a tree in the wilderness, Jezebel would have succeeded in both silencing a prophet of the Lord and ending his life prematurely. But Elijah's story didn't end there.

> Then as he lay and slept under a broom tree, suddenly an angel touched him, and said to him, "Arise and eat." Then he looked, and there by his head was a cake baked on coals, and a jar of water. So he ate and drank, and lay down again. And the angel of the LORD came back the second time, and touched him, and said, "Arise and eat, because the journey is too great for you." So he arose, and ate and drank; and he went in the strength of that food forty days and forty nights as far as Horeb, the mountain of God.

And there he went into a cave, and spent the night in that place; and behold, the word of the LORD came to him, and He said to him, "What are you doing here, Elijah?"

So he said, "I have been very zealous for the LORD God of hosts; for the children of Israel have forsaken Your covenant, torn down Your altars, and killed Your prophets with the sword. I alone am left; and they seek to take my life."

—1 KINGS 19:1–10

After all he had been through, Elijah had to be exhausted, drained. Because of that, he was susceptible to succumbing to the attacks of the enemy. But the Lord wasn't finished with him yet. Just as He did when Elijah was in the wilderness the first time, the Lord supernaturally provided for Elijah, sending an angel with food and water. The Lord recognized that Elijah was feeling overwhelmed, and He provided the rest, food, and encouragement he needed for his journey.

Elijah left the broom tree and journeyed to Mount Horeb, even farther away in the wilderness. Even though the Lord once again worked miracles on Elijah's behalf, he was still stuck in a pit of self-pity. When the Lord asked Elijah what he was doing on the mountain, Elijah aired his woe-is-me tale. He was so caught in self-pity that he exaggerated his situation. He knew that the children of Israel on Mount Carmel had repented and turned back to the Lord. He also knew that Obadiah had saved one hundred other prophets from being executed by Jezebel.

When we are battling the issues in our minds, it is all too easy to fall into self-pity. It is all too easy to think we are alone, that we are the only ones fighting the battle, that no one else is struggling the way we are. Prophets are human and subject to the same passions and emotions as everyone else. Prophets must operate in the strength of the Spirit of God, but they still need encouragement and prayer.

When the attack of the enemy leaves you feeling overwhelmed, run to the wilderness. Hide yourself away with the Lord again so He can renew your strength. Hide yourself away so you can be reminded of all the great things He has done for you. Hide yourself away so you can fellowship with the Lord and spend time talking to Him and hearing from Him. That is what Elijah did.

> Then He said, "Go out, and stand on the mountain before the LORD." And behold, the LORD passed by, and a great and strong wind tore into the mountains and broke the rocks in pieces before the LORD, but the LORD was not in the wind; and after the wind an earthquake, but the LORD was not in the earthquake; and after the earthquake a fire, but the LORD was not in the fire; and after the fire a still small voice.
>
> So it was, when Elijah heard it, that he wrapped his face in his mantle and went out and stood in the entrance of the cave. Suddenly a voice came to him, and said, "What are you doing here, Elijah?"
>
> And he said, "I have been very zealous for the LORD God of hosts; because the children of Israel have forsaken Your covenant, torn down Your altars, and killed Your prophets with the sword. I alone am left; and they seek to take my life."
>
> Then the LORD said to him: "Go, return on your way to the Wilderness of Damascus; and when you arrive, anoint Hazael as king over Syria. Also you shall anoint Jehu the son of Nimshi as king over Israel. And Elisha the son of Shaphat of Abel Meholah you shall anoint as prophet in your place. It shall be that whoever escapes the sword of Hazael, Jehu will kill; and whoever escapes the sword of Jehu, Elisha will kill. Yet I have reserved

seven thousand in Israel, all whose knees have not bowed
to Baal, and every mouth that has not kissed him."
—1 KINGS 19:11–18

When we are feeling overwhelmed—when we are running
scared or wallowing in self-pity—we need to get to the place
where we can hear the still small voice of the Lord. For even
when we are struggling, He still sees us, He still loves us, and
He still has a purpose for us in the earth.

God didn't condemn Elijah for his struggle. He showed him
compassion, met his physical needs, encouraged his heart, and
still spoke to him. He also let Elijah know that his assignment
wasn't finished yet, and the Lord gave Elijah the plan to fulfill
his assignment.

Guarding against pitfalls and hindrances is essential for every
prophet, even those who exhibit the fervent spirit of Elijah.
The very qualities that make Elijah a powerful prophet—zeal,
courage, and a strong connection to God—can also become
stumbling blocks if not carefully managed.

The burden of being a prophet can be heavy at times, and
there may be moments of discouragement or feeling overwhelmed. Self-pity is a trap that diverts the prophet's focus
from God's mission to their personal struggles and challenges.
When self-pity takes hold, the prophet's effectiveness in delivering God's message may diminish as they become preoccu-
pied with their own feelings of inadequacy or victimhood.
Embracing humility and recognizing that the prophetic calling
is not about personal comfort but about serving God's purpose
will guard against self-pity. Prophets must continually realign
their focus on the divine mission and rely on God's strength to
endure any hardships they encounter.

The zeal and courage exhibited by the spirit of Elijah can
sometimes lead to a dangerous sense of self-importance—the
pitfall of pride. Pride may cause the prophet to believe their

insights and opinions are infallible, distorting the divine message they are meant to convey. A prideful prophet may become resistant to feedback or correction, believing they alone possess the truth. Cultivating humility and recognizing that the prophet is a vessel for God's message, not the source of it, is crucial. By staying open to the counsel of wise mentors and fellow believers, prophets help prevent pride from clouding their prophetic vision.

Even the most courageous prophets can grapple with fear, especially when confronting powerful opposition or delivering difficult truths. Fear can paralyze the prophet, preventing them from boldly speaking the word of the Lord. Trusting in God's sovereignty and promises allows prophets to overcome fear. They must lean on God's strength and not their own, knowing that the Lord is their protector and sustainer in the face of adversity.

Cultivating self-awareness can help prophets avoid pitfalls. Being mindful of their emotions and motivations empowers prophets to recognize when self-pity, pride, or fear starts to creep into their hearts. Self-awareness allows them to address these hindrances promptly and seek God's help in overcoming them.

Dependence on God is also vital in avoiding prophetic pitfalls. The journey of a prophet is not one to walk alone. Reliance on God's wisdom, guidance, and strength is essential. Prophets must maintain a deep connection to God through prayer, studying His Word, and seeking His direction in all things.

So while the spirit of Elijah exemplifies zeal, courage, and a strong connection to God, it also reminds us of the importance of guarding against pitfalls that can hinder the effectiveness of God's messengers. By cultivating humility, self-awareness, and complete dependence on God, today's Elijah prophets can navigate these challenges, stay true to their calling, and effectively deliver the divine message to the world.

Prophets often deal with fragmented souls. They deal with

fear. They deal with rejection. They deal with self-pity. Prophets deal with fragmented souls due to the intense spiritual and emotional challenges they face in their prophetic ministry. The calling of a prophet involves receiving and conveying divine messages, confronting sin and unrighteousness, and interceding on behalf of others. These responsibilities can take a toll on a prophet's soul, leading to fragmentation in several ways:

Emotional burden—Prophets are often called to deliver messages of judgment, repentance, and warning to both individuals and nations. Witnessing the consequences of sin and disobedience can affect their emotions deeply, leading to feelings of grief, sorrow, and burden for the people they are called to serve.

Spiritual warfare—Prophets are on the front lines of spiritual battles, engaging in intense spiritual warfare against dark forces that seek to oppose and hinder God's work. This constant spiritual warfare can result in soul weariness and fragmentation.

Rejection and isolation—Prophets may face rejection and opposition, even from their own communities and religious establishments. This rejection can lead to feelings of isolation and loneliness, causing fragmentation in their emotional and relational well-being.

Identification with others' pain—Prophets often empathize deeply with the pain and suffering of those they minister to. They carry the burdens of others, and this can lead to their souls being fragmented by the weight of others' struggles.

Carrying the heart of God—Prophets are called to carry the heart of God for His people. This means experiencing God's love, compassion, and righteous anger toward sin. Carrying such intense

emotions can lead to fragmentation as they
navigate between their own emotions and those
of God.

Seeing the unseen—Prophets often have visions and
encounters with the spiritual realm, witnessing
both the glory of God and the schemes of
the enemy. These supernatural experiences
can be overwhelming and may result in soul
fragmentation as they try to comprehend and
process the mysteries of the spiritual realm.

Personal weakness and vulnerability—Prophets, like
any other human beings, are not immune to
personal weaknesses and vulnerabilities. Their
struggles with sin, doubt, and personal challenges
can further contribute to fragmented souls.

Despite these challenges, prophets have the assurance of God's presence and the empowerment of the Holy Spirit to sustain them. The process of dealing with fragmented souls often involves seeking God's healing, restoration, and renewal through prayer, worship, and the Word of God. Additionally, support from a loving and understanding community can play a significant role in helping prophets navigate the complexities of their prophetic ministry and find wholeness in their souls.

The powers of darkness will come against prophets. The goal is to shut their mouths. That is why Satan comes against them with rejection, fear of man, pride, self-pity, and even premature death. He will do anything and everything to try to shut their mouths. As prophets, we have to be mindful of those things. Just because your gift is working does not mean you don't have to walk in humility and relationship with the Lord, that you don't have to have godly character, and that you don't need to be diligent to shut the doors against the demonic attacks coming at you. Because of the surge in witchcraft, we need to be diligent about decreeing the Word and breaking curses off our lives.

The litmus test for a true prophet is not the accuracy of their prophecy. The Word says you will know a tree by its fruit. A true prophet will not bear fruits of unrighteousness. A true prophet is not only accurate but also bears the fruits of righteousness.

Spiritual gifts are just that—they are gifts. God doesn't give you a gift and then take it back just because you are struggling or made a mistake. But it is up to you how you use that gift. There are people who have spiritual gifts that use them for the works of darkness. You need to choose whom you will yield your spirit to—the Lord or the enemy. When you yield your spirit to the Lord, you will bear the fruits of righteousness.

That is why wilderness time is critical. It both prepares you for your assignment and refreshes and restores you when you have been wounded in the battle. So guard your heart; if you find yourself facing the spirit of Jezebel and falling for any prophetic pitfalls, get to the wilderness again. Give yourself time hidden away with the Lord so you can hear His still small voice and get ready for the next phase of your assignment.

WHO'S YOUR ENEMY?

When the attacks come—and they will—you need to recognize who your real enemy is. While the attack may be coming directly from a human being, whether someone in the church or someone outside the church, that person isn't the real enemy. It is the powers of darkness and Satan who want to keep us in bondage, to keep people turning away from the Lord.

So don't return an attack to a human being. The battle is in the spirit, not the natural. Ephesians 6:12 reminds us, "For we do not wrestle against flesh and blood, but against principalities, against powers, against the rulers of the darkness of this age, against spiritual hosts of wickedness in the heavenly places." Curses come from the power of darkness. And when we return those curses, they need to be returned to the originator—the devil and his demons—not to a person.

Jesus said, "Love your enemies, bless those who curse you, do good to those who hate you, and pray for those who spitefully use you and persecute you" (Matt. 5:44). We have been called to bless and not curse. Since we are called to turn the hearts of people back to the Lord, it is all the more important that we remember to bless our enemies rather than curse them since it is the kindness of the Lord that draws people to repentance.

The essence of the prophetic anointing is the nature of the lion:

> Surely the Lord God does nothing, unless He reveals His secret to His servants the prophets. A lion has roared! Who will not fear? The Lord GOD has spoken! Who can but prophesy?
>
> —AMOS 3:7–8

The Elijah anointing comes to restore the roar of prophetic lions back to the church. It comes to restore boldness.

As prophets of the Lord, we are not zoo lions, caged by tradition and afraid to speak with the cutting edge and zeal of the Lord.

We are not circus lions, a source of entertainment and jokes, performing religious tricks and manipulating people with illusions.

We are kingdom lions who roar with the voice of the Lord. Psalm 29 says the voice of the Lord is powerful and full of majesty. It breaks the cedars and shakes the wilderness. When the prophets of the Lord roar the word of the Lord, things change—chains and curses are broken, hearts are turned, miracles are done, and people are restored. When the Elijah prophets roar, the spirit of Jezebel, principalities, powers of darkness, demonic spirits, and anything else the enemy sends to attack us will be defeated!

PART III
RESTORATION

Chapter 11

Miracles of Restoration

MIRACLES REVEAL THE character of God. A miracle is a remarkable occurrence that surpasses the boundaries of natural laws, brought about by divine intervention. Miracles are extraordinary signs of God's presence and power in our lives. These supernatural events go beyond scientific explanation and the usual expectations of the natural world. Miracles are divine manifestations that demonstrate the authority and transcendence of our Almighty God.

These miraculous acts serve as clear demonstrations of God's involvement in human affairs. Miracles can take on various forms, such as miraculous healings, unexpected changes in circumstances, divine protection from harm, or the fulfillment of seemingly impossible prayers and requests. As prophetic Christians, we recognize that miracles are a testament to God's love and compassion for His creation and a reminder of His divine presence in our lives.

A miracle is a work wrought by the divine power of God for a purpose beyond the reach of man. When God works miracles, He is awakening dreams and visions in our hearts—and the purpose of that is beyond our reach. When God works miracles, He is showing Himself strong on our behalf. When God performs wonders, He is showing us His unconditional and unfailing love. When God opens up the door to the miraculous, He is showing us divine favor. When God works miracles, He is showing us He is God.

The restoration miracles Elijah performed were about restoring the human condition, closing the door on poverty, and connecting with people's real needs. It is important that Elijah prophets don't disconnect from the natural. Prophets walking in the spirit and power of Elijah need to learn how to demystify the prophetic realm. Sometimes people are actually physically hungry, and that kind of hunger can make it hard for them to hear and accept the word of the Lord. There doesn't always need to be a prayer movement when providing someone a meal can meet their needs and enable them to receive the lovingkindness of God. Again, the Elijah anointing is about both word and deed. It is about restoring honor and grace to the prophetic ministry.

When we are moving in the spirit and power of Elijah, miracles of restoration are part of our assignment as agents of change. We have been chosen for this season to bring the favor, the power, and the plenty of God to a world in need. We have access to the realm of miraculous provision, overflow, and abundance. As Elijah prophets, we become distribution centers for the more-than-enough blessings of the Lord. Get ready to move in the miraculous.

MIRACLE OF MULTIPLICATION

The first miracle of restoration the Lord performed by the word of Elijah was a miracle of multiplication.

During the drought, the Lord sent Elijah to the widow of

Zarephath after his time in the wilderness at the Brook Cherith. We already looked at Elijah's interactions with the widow as an illustration of how the assignment of Elijah prophets is about both word and deed. The widow was in dire straits. Between her widowhood and the drought that was affecting both her and the people who might typically help her, the widow had lost hope.

When someone has a natural or practical need, it can become all-consuming. It is hard to hear from the Lord when your stomach is aching with hunger because you haven't eaten in two days, or when you know your children are hungry. It is hard to have faith in God's provision when your six-year-old's shoes have gotten so small they hurt her feet, but you can't afford new ones. It's hard to believe God really cares about you when you have been looking for a job for a month without success, and you are about to lose your home. When you are facing real-life, day-to-day, in-your-face struggles, it is hard to have hope.

But we need hope. The Scripture says, "Hope deferred makes the heart sick" (Prov. 13:12). Hopelessness brings sorrow. Hopelessness brings defeat. Hopelessness undermines faith.

That is why Elijahs operate in both word and deed. The Book of James asks, "If a brother or sister is naked and destitute of daily food, and one of you says to them, 'Depart in peace, be warmed and filled,' but you do not give them the things which are needed for the body, what does it profit?" (2:15–16). That is why the Elijah anointing carries the power for miracles of restoration—for when physical needs are met, hope and faith are restored.

When Elijah asked the widow to bring him a morsel of bread in her hand, she only had a handful of flour and a very small amount of oil at home. To put that in perspective, a handful is about half a cup of flour, but the typical bread recipe calls for at least two cups of flour. The widow was literally scraping the bottom of her barrel of flour. She was facing death by starvation for both herself and her son.

A handful was all she had, but with God's hand at work, a handful was all she needed.

The miracle of the multiplication was about God's care for us. Sometimes we focus so much on what we lack that we overlook God's power to work with what we have. When Jesus told His disciples to feed a crowd that numbered probably at least fifteen thousand (there were five thousand men plus all the women and children), the disciples must have thought He had lost His mind. How could they feed that many people? Even if they had enough money to buy food for that many people, they were in a deserted area, so there was no place to buy food. The disciples had five loaves and two fish, but instead of looking at what they had and what Jesus could do with it, they focused on the lack. But God is a God of miracles. He is a God of multiplication. Jesus took those loaves and fish, blessed them, and had the disciples start handing out supper. Every single person ate until they were filled, and there were even leftovers for the next day.

The miracle of the flour and oil was also about trusting God every day. When you take your focus off your lack and put it on God's power to use what you have, you are choosing to trust. You are choosing to take what you have and sow it—to give it, to share it. You are allowing God to take everything you have and multiply it. That is exactly what happened with the widow of Zarephath. She offered her flour and oil, she sowed a seed by making a small cake for Elijah in an act of faith, and God multiplied the flour and oil so that neither ever ran out. She took her handful of flour and put it into the hand of Elijah, and the hand of the Lord moved on her behalf.

We are in a season of multiplication. God is going to multiply every seed you sow by faith, everything you've given. God keeps good records, and there is no lack in His kingdom. God's children are not going to be bound by the spirit of poverty. When the enemy comes in, trying to keep you staring at your lack in the natural, you just keep sowing your seeds of faith, trusting God day by day. I don't care what the enemy is saying to you; God will not allow you to go hungry. I decree that this is a season of great multiplication. I decree you will not run out. A continual and perpetual blessing will follow you, your children, and your children's children because of the seed you sow now.

There is one other key thing I want you to see about the miracle of multiplication. The Lord multiplied flour, or bread, and oil. Bread represents the Word of God. Oil represents the Holy Spirit. When we are walking in the spirit and power of Elijah, we need both the Word and the Spirit multiplied in our lives.

We need to be feasting on the Word of God—having a hearty meal from the Bible every day. We need to be reading it, memorizing it, meditating on it, studying it, speaking it, and writing it on the tablets of our hearts. We need the Word of God to be multiplied in our hearts and minds.

We also need to remember that Jesus is the Word. John 1:1 says, "In the beginning was the Word, and the Word was with God, and the Word was God." And the day after the feeding of the five thousand, Jesus said:

> I am the bread of life. He who comes to Me shall never hunger, and he who believes in Me shall never thirst....I am the bread of life. Your fathers ate the manna in the wilderness, and are dead. This is the bread which comes down from heaven, that one may eat of it and not die. I am the living bread which came down from heaven. If anyone eats of this bread, he will live forever; and the bread that I shall give is My flesh, which I shall give for the life of the world.
>
> —JOHN 6:35, 48–51

Jesus is the living Word. We need Him to be multiplied in our lives too. We need to become more and more like Him every day, bearing the fruits of righteousness and doing the greater works He assigned us to do.

Not only do we need the Word multiplied in our lives, but we also need the precious oil of the Holy Spirit multiplied in our lives. As Elijah prophets, we need to be in tune with the Holy Spirit. We need to grow more and more sensitive to His voice, to His direction, to His unction. We need to be anointed with fresh oil. We need the Lord to pour out His Spirit on us.

> And it shall come to pass afterward that I will pour out My Spirit on all flesh; your sons and your daughters shall prophesy, your old men shall dream dreams, your young men shall see visions. And also on My menservants and on My maidservants I will pour out My Spirit in those days.
>
> —JOEL 2:28–29

The Hebrew word translated "pour out" means to pour out, to spill forth, to expend, to sprawl out, to gush out, to pour into a mold. The word doesn't mean there will just be a few drops poured into you. When you pour something into a mold, you fill it completely. We need to be filled completely with the Holy Spirit. We need to be filled with "the Spirit of the LORD...the Spirit of wisdom and understanding, the Spirit of counsel and might, the Spirit of knowledge and of the fear of the LORD" (Isa. 11:1–2). We need multiplication of the oil.

As the Lord anointed Elijah in ancient times to multiply the limited resources of the widow, so He is anointing you, His chosen vessel, to bring forth supernatural provision and abundance in the lives of His people.

In the midst of scarcity and lack, do not fear, for the power of God is upon you. Just as Elijah spoke with authority and faith, I decree that your words shall carry the weight of heaven.

As you speak in alignment with God's will, resources shall multiply in the hands of those in need.

I declare the anointing of Elijah upon you to release supernatural multiplication in all areas of life. Your prayers and intercessions shall bring divine sustenance, not only in physical needs but also in spiritual growth, emotional healing, and divine direction.

No longer shall you be bound by limitations, for the Spirit of the Lord is upon you. Your life shall be a conduit of God's miraculous provision, and as you walk in obedience, His abundance shall overflow.

Just as the widow's jars of flour and oil did not run dry, so shall the resources and blessings in your life be replenished continually. Your faith and trust in the Lord's promises shall be rewarded, and you shall witness the glory of God's miraculous multiplication.

Receive this prophetic decree, for the anointing of Elijah rests upon you. Step into the realm of supernatural abundance, for God's hand is upon you to release His provision and blessings beyond measure. Go forth in the power of the Spirit, for you are an instrument of divine multiplication in the earth.

MIRACLE OF SUSTAINING

The second miracle of restoration was a miracle of sustaining. This miracle was when God caused the ravens to feed Elijah. Remember, the raven was known as an unclean or dirty bird. It was an unconventional way to provide for Elijah and sustain him, but I believe when God begins to speak to systems and men, their whole nature begins to change. That is why the miracle of the raven was so important.

Think about it. Ravens are scavengers. They will eat up everything in sight. They will eat everything from small animals to carrion to eggs to berries to bugs. Any wild animal bringing food to Elijah would have been miraculous, but the fact that it was a raven is even more miraculous because the nature of the raven is to eat everything. The raven wasn't bringing Elijah something that it never would have eaten anyway.

There may have been ravens around you trying to bite off your stuff. Ravens may have been trying to devour what has been feeding you, whether physically, emotionally, or spiritually. But God works miracles to sustain you. He is going to command those ravens to feed you rather than scavenge from you. God can command both the clean and the unclean to sustain you. He is the Lord over all creation, so He can use unconventional methods to supernaturally provide for you.

The miracle with the ravens was not the only time the Lord miraculously sustained Elijah because it was not the only time Elijah was in the wilderness. Remember, Elijah ended up in the wilderness again after Jezebel threatened his life in the aftermath of the showdown at Mount Carmel. And because of Elijah's mental and emotional state when he headed into the wilderness—he was so discouraged, depressed, and downtrodden that he prayed to die—I am sure he didn't bring forty-plus days of provisions with him.

Yet despite Elijah's attitude—despite his struggles, fear, sorrow, and lack of faith—the Lord still miraculously provided for him. He headed into the wilderness, prayed to die, and fell asleep underneath a tree. Then an angel touched him and told him to get up and eat, and Elijah saw a coal-baked cake of bread and some water. Elijah took another nap, and then the same thing happened again. Those two angelic meals were enough to sustain him for forty days and forty nights as he journeyed farther into the wilderness to Horeb, the mountain of God.

The tree Elijah took shelter under when he entered the wilderness for the second time was a broom tree. It grows in the deserts of the Arabian Peninsula. Its roots are actually edible, so Elijah did have a potential food source, although it would have taken some effort on his part to dig up the roots. But only poor people ever ate the roots of broom trees because they are very bitter. In large amounts, the roots will also make you sick.

So when the Lord once again miraculously provided food to sustain Elijah, He was once again showing His care. He was showing Elijah that He loved him. Think about it: Elijah was wallowing in self-pity. He was dealing with fear, despair, discouragement, doubt, and many other emotions the enemy was firing at him. He didn't need to eat something that might make him sick. He needed to be refreshed, renewed, and restored. The last thing he needed was bitter roots, either natural or spiritual.

When Moses was warning the children of Israel about idolatry, he said:

> I make this covenant and this oath, not with you alone, but with him who stands here with us today before the Lord our God, as well as with him who is not here with us today (for you know that we dwelt in the land of Egypt and that we came through the nations which you passed by, and you saw their abominations and their idols which were among them—wood and stone and silver and gold); so that there may not be among you man or woman or family or tribe, whose heart turns away today from the Lord our God, to go and serve the gods of these nations, and that there may not be among you a root bearing bitterness or wormwood.
>
> —Deuteronomy 29:14–18

Moses identified idolatry as hearts turning away from the Lord and bitter roots springing up. And that is exactly what the enemy wanted to happen to Elijah. Elijah had experienced a great victory of the Lord against the devil, and the devil didn't want that to ever happen again. Satan wanted Elijah to be so discouraged and defeated that the prophet called to turn hearts back to the Lord turned away from the Lord himself and ended up with a heart full of bitterness. But again, the Lord knew Elijah's heart. He knew the attacks he was facing. He knew how much he was struggling. So instead of allowing Elijah to have to eat bitter roots, the Lord provided an angelic meal for His weary prophet. The Lord wasn't going to allow Elijah to have either physical or spiritual bitter roots.

That is the power of God. That is the love of God. That is the care of God.

MIRACLE OF RESURRECTION

The last miracle of restoration was the miracle of resurrection. The widow of Zarephath, the same one who saw her flour and oil multiplied, had a son. But her son got sick and died.

Elijah took her son and carried him up to the room he was staying in. He cried out to the Lord for the life of the widow's son, and the Lord heard and answered. The boy was resurrected and returned to the arms of his mother. It was a miracle of resurrection.

The supernatural power of God to resurrect is an awe-inspiring and wondrous display of His divine authority over life and death. It showcases His limitless ability to bring back what was lost, to revive the lifeless, and to breathe hope into the hopeless.

In the account of Elijah, we witness this remarkable manifestation of God's resurrection power. Through the prophet's intercession and unwavering faith, God breathed life back into the dead child, defying all natural laws and limitations. This incredible event serves as a powerful testament to the miraculous nature of our heavenly Father. It reminds us that His dominion extends beyond the realms of our understanding, and His ability to restore and renew knows no bounds.

The resurrection power of God is not limited to the past but remains accessible to us today. In times of despair and darkness, when all hope seems lost, we can call upon the same God who raised the widow's son to life. He is the God of miracles, and His supernatural power is ever available to those who believe and call upon His name.

This truth invites us to approach God with boldness and expectancy, knowing that He holds the keys to life and death in His hands. Let us stand in awe of His resurrection power, trusting in His unfailing love and capacity to bring forth new life even in the most dire circumstances.

As we witness God's supernatural power to resurrect, our faith is strengthened and our hearts are filled with wonder and gratitude. May this miraculous display of His authority lead us to a deeper reverence for our Almighty Creator and inspire us to seek His resurrection power in our lives and the lives of others. In Him, we find the source of eternal hope and the assurance of a future that goes beyond the boundaries of this temporal world.

But the miracle of resurrection wasn't just about the boy coming back to life, although that was indeed miraculous. It was also about the resurrection of the widow's faith. We can imagine all the attacks on her faith she had faced up to that point in her life. While we don't know all the details of her struggles, we do know some. She was a widow, so she knew what it meant to have loved and lost. She knew what it meant to grieve. She knew what it meant to be overwhelmed by sorrow. She knew what it meant to lose her provider and the provider for her son. She knew what it meant to go hungry. She knew what it meant to suffer. She knew what it meant to be afraid. She knew what it meant to be down to the last handful of flour and the last little bit of oil. She knew what it meant to face death by starvation, both for herself and her son. Is it any wonder that her faith had been shaken?

Yet even in the midst of shaken faith, she still strived to take steps of faith. She still sowed seeds of faith. She recognized that Elijah was a man of God, so she still believed in God. But she might not have been so sure that God was for her rather than against her. She might have wondered whether God was multiplying the flour and oil just because Elijah was there, thinking the miracle might end when Elijah left, leaving her right back where she was before he came. So when her son died, it could have very well been the last nail in the coffin of her faith.

But then Elijah raised her son from the dead. Her son was resurrected and restored to her. And her faith was resurrected and restored too, for she was then able to say not only that Elijah was a man of God but also that "the word of the LORD in your mouth is the truth" (1 Kings 17:24). The miracle of resurrection opened her heart to not just hear the word of the Lord but also to receive it.

This particular miracle goes beyond the widow and her son though. A son was raised back to life, and that points toward the calling of Elijah prophets to "turn the hearts of the fathers to the children, and the hearts of the children to their fathers" (Mal. 4:6). The Lord is in the business of resurrecting and restoring families.

The enemy may be trying to kill your children, either physically or spiritually. But God is in the resurrection business. The devil may have stolen your children away so that they are walking zombies, unaware of the divine purpose and calling on their lives, but the Lord is the Lord of restoration miracles.

As prophets of the Lord, we have access to the Lord's resurrection power. The Spirit of God dwells in us, and the Spirit of God raised Christ from the dead. Romans 8:11 says, "But if the Spirit of Him who raised Jesus from the dead dwells in you, He who raised Christ from the dead will also give life to your mortal bodies through His Spirit who dwells in you." Elijah moved with the unction of the Holy Spirit, but we have a big advantage over him. During the days of Elijah, while the Holy

Spirit was already at work in the world, He had not yet come to dwell with us and in us. That didn't happen until after Jesus died, rose again, and ascended into heaven to sit at the right hand of the Father. You have the Holy Spirit dwelling inside of you. That means you have access to Holy Ghost power 24/7.

It is time for Elijah prophets to rise up and use that resurrection power on whatever it is that needs to be brought back to life—marriages, relationships, faith, purpose, dreams, destinies, callings, and so forth. It is time for the prophets of the Lord to rise up and call upon the Spirit of God to work miracles of restoration—in our families, our churches, our communities, our cities, and our nation. It is time for those walking in the spirit and power of Elijah to work miracles that will come against the spirit of Jezebel warring against this nation and turn hearts back to the one true God. It is time for families to be restored, for the hearts of fathers to be turned back to their children and for the hearts of children to be turned back to their fathers.

I will say it again: there is miraculous power available from the Spirit of the Lord, and it is time for Elijahs to rise up and put a demand on that power. It is time to release a whole new level of faith.

God is bestowing His anointing upon prophets in the likeness of Elijah, gifting them with powerful mantles to perform miracles. Through these miraculous demonstrations, God's intention is to rekindle and revive the sense of awe and wonder within the hearts of the church. These anointed prophets will be vessels through which God's divine power and intervention are made manifest, inspiring believers to witness His greatness and sovereignty.

In the spirit of Elijah, these prophets will carry the mantle of divine authority, exhibiting the zeal, courage, and strong connection to God that characterized the prophet Elijah. As they walk in alignment with God's will and operate under His anointing, they will be instrumental in bringing forth extraordinary and supernatural occurrences that go beyond human comprehension or scientific explanation.

These miraculous acts will serve as signs of God's presence and His desire to restore awe and reverence in the hearts of His people. The church will witness physical healings, deliverance from bondage, restoration of broken lives, and encounters with the divine that will ignite a fresh sense of wonder and amazement among believers.

Through these anointed prophets, God will demonstrate His authority over the natural world, showing that nothing is impossible for Him. As the church witnesses these mighty works, it will be drawn closer to God, deepening its faith and inspiring a greater devotion to the One who performs such extraordinary acts.

In this divine season, the prophetic ministry will play a pivotal role in bringing about spiritual renewal, awakening, and restoration in the hearts of believers. God's anointing on Elijah-type prophets will serve as a catalyst for revival, ushering in a time of awe-filled worship, steadfast faith, and a greater hunger for a deeper relationship with the Almighty. The church will be stirred to wholeheartedly pursue God's presence, and His glory will be magnified in their midst.

Chapter 12

Turning Hearts

THE ELIJAH ANOINTING comes to confront fatherlessness in our generation. As I mentioned in the introduction, fatherlessness is at epidemic levels in our nation. According to the US Census Bureau, as of 2022, there were almost 18.4 million children living in homes without a father present.[1] To put that in perspective, that number is more than double the population of New York City.

Children raised in homes without a father are four times more likely to live in poverty, seven times more likely to face teenage pregnancy, more likely to have behavior problems, more likely to drop out of school, more likely to abuse alcohol or drugs, more likely to commit criminal acts, more likely to end up in prison, and more likely to be abused.[2] The enemy's fingerprints are all over the fatherlessness issue. But the fatherlessness issue is one the Father wants to address.

In the divine unfolding of the end-time revival, a powerful echo resounds, connecting the essence of Elijah's historic ministry to the prophetic words of Malachi. This glorious revival shall be characterized by a profound manifestation of God's power, confirming Elijah's message with the spirit of prophecy, just as witnessed in the days of old.

In the prophetic words of Malachi, a key message emerges—a message of turning hearts. God's heart for children and the fatherless takes center stage, drawing attention to their needs and well-being in the end-time purposes of God to see justice done in the earth.

> Behold, I will send you Elijah the prophet before the coming of the great and dreadful day of the LORD. And he will turn the hearts of the fathers to the children, and the hearts of the children to their fathers, lest I come and strike the earth with a curse.
> —MALACHI 4:5–6

In this miraculous season, fathers, both natural and spiritual, will experience a divine transformation. The turning of their hearts shall herald a time of abundant generosity as powerful men relinquish their resources for the sake of children. This act of selflessness transcends worldly influence as fathers pour into the lives of those who cannot offer anything in return.

The fatherless, those who lack a paternal figure in their lives, have a special place in God's heart. They are not merely orphans but souls deserving of love, care, and guidance. God's power, as witnessed in the ministry of Elijah, will be directed toward these vulnerable ones as He draws attention to their needs, both physical and emotional.

In this momentous revival, let us embrace the call to turn our hearts—to extend love and support to the fatherless, to mentor and guide the younger generation, and to cherish the sacred bond within our families. As we heed this divine mandate, we become vessels of God's love and instruments of

His end-time justice, igniting a transformation that transcends time and echoes throughout eternity.

THE FATHERING SPIRIT

God is a Father. It is one of His primary roles. Because of that, the fatherlessness issue grieves His heart. The Lord has always had compassion for the fatherless—it didn't just start as the fatherlessness epidemic spread. The Torah, or the Law, references care for the fatherless twelve times. The Word says the Lord "administers justice for the fatherless," is "the helper of the fatherless," is "a father of the fatherless," and "relieves the fatherless," and in Him "the fatherless finds mercy" (Deut. 10:18; Ps. 10:14; 68:5; 146:9; Hos. 14:3).

Part of the role of a father is to identify and name his child and bring forth the destiny of the child. Because of the lack of fathers, both natural and spiritual, many children are growing up without the familial connections that provide a foundation for pursuing their God-given purposes and fulfilling the divine destinies on their lives. The Elijah anointing carries a fathering spirit that sets the lonely in families and calls the generations back to their identities and destinies in the kingdom of God.

In the tapestry of end-time revival, the turning of fathers' hearts becomes a multifaceted mission:

- The turning of natural fathers' hearts to their families is a divine restoration of the family unit. Fathers will embrace their roles with love and devotion, providing nurturing environments for their children to grow and flourish.

- Spiritual fathers and mothers in the church will take up the mantle of mentorship, pouring into the younger generation. They will pass down the wisdom and faith of generations past, empowering the next wave of believers to rise and carry the torch of truth. The call to turn the hearts of spiritual fathers and mothers in the church is a divine mandate to mentor and nurture the younger generation. Guided by God's power, spiritual leaders shall embrace their roles as mentors, imparting wisdom and sharing their faith journey. As they invest in the spiritual growth and development of the next generation, a powerful transformation takes root within the church, fostering unity, purpose, and a continuous legacy of faith.

• Fathers in society—be it in the church, government, marketplace, or any realm of influence—will extend their care and protection to the fatherless. The turning of their hearts will set in motion a wave of compassion and justice, ensuring the well-being of those in need.

As the spirit and power of Elijah find resonance in the hearts of the faithful, a divine transformation sweeps across the land. The end-time revival, characterized by Elijah's ministry, draws near, bringing forth a season of divine reconciliation, love, and restoration. In the vast tapestry of society, encompassing the realms of the church, government, marketplace, and beyond, a profound transformation beckons. The power of God's love seeks to turn the hearts of fathers toward the fatherless. Fathers in positions of influence and authority shall extend their arms of compassion and protection to those lacking paternal guidance, ensuring that the needs of the vulnerable are met and their voices are heard.

In this convergence of divine power and human response, the end-time purposes of God to see justice done find their focal point in the well-being of children. As the hearts of powerful men turn toward these innocent souls, a wave of transformation begins to ripple through families, communities, and societies at large. This outpouring of compassion and care reflects the very heart of God, who calls on His children to become instruments of His love and justice.

Those who are most vulnerable and in need of a righteous Judge's intervention are often the fatherless—children who are abused, exploited, or neglected, particularly within the dark shadows of human trafficking. The fatherless find themselves in precarious positions, susceptible to various forms of exploitation and injustice. Within the grim reality of human trafficking, they become victims of unspeakable horrors, stripped of their innocence and subjected to unimaginable suffering. Neglected by society, they face a lack of care, guidance, and protection, leaving them exposed to a world that fails to acknowledge their worth. God's heart is deeply moved by their plight, and His justice demands swift action to protect and uphold their rights.

In the Scriptures, we find divine admonitions against those who exploit the vulnerable, including widows and orphans. Malachi 3:5 stands as a poignant reminder of God's stance on such matters: "'So I will come to put you on trial. I will be quick to testify against sorcerers, adulterers, and perjurers, against those who defraud laborers of their wages, who oppress the widows and the fatherless, and deprive the foreigners among you of justice, but do not fear me,' says the Lord Almighty" (NIV).

God's justice is not just a means of retribution but a merciful call to stop those who perpetrate evil upon the fatherless and the marginalized. In His divine wisdom, God raises His gavel of justice to protect the innocent and to hold the perpetrators accountable for their actions. The purpose of judgment is to bring an end to the exploitation and abuse, to cease the oppression and neglect, and to restore dignity and hope to the fatherless.

We are called to echo God's heart for justice, standing as advocates for the fatherless and all who are oppressed. Our mission is to shine a light into the darkness, to expose the hidden atrocities of human trafficking, and to extend a helping hand to those in need. By actively engaging in the fight against exploitation, we become vessels of God's justice, instruments of change in a world yearning for redemption.

In this journey of justice, let us remember the words of the prophet Isaiah: "Learn to do right; seek justice. Defend the oppressed. Take up the cause of the fatherless; plead the case of the widow" (Isa. 1:17, NIV). As we stand united in the pursuit of justice for the fatherless, we exemplify the love and compassion of our righteous Judge, heralding a future where the vulnerable are shielded, the oppressed are liberated, and the fatherless find solace and security in the embrace of a caring society.

THE HEARTS OF FATHERS AND CHILDREN

Elijah prophets are called to turn the hearts of fathers to their children and the hearts of children to their fathers. They carry a fathering spirit. They carry a mantle of restoration for families. But in order for families to be restored, in order for fathers' hearts to turn to their children, there must first be another turning—the turning of hearts back to the Lord. That is why the message of repentance and reformation is vital for those with the spirit and power of Elijah.

Elijah preached messages that turned hearts. He was a preacher of righteousness. To take up this part of Elijah's mantle, we must pray, "God, let me preach the message no one wants to preach!" These are messages full of power, passion, holiness, fire, and righteousness. They are messages that produce signs and wonders. They are accompanied by prayer and intercession. The messages are confrontational and truth-telling. They are messages emblazoned with the zeal of the Lord that builds men rather than just blessing them. Proclaiming the vengeance of God on idolatry, the messages produce God's justice in the earth.

The Elijah anointing turns the hearts of fathers to their children and the hearts of children to their fathers. It is a call to restore relationships between fathers and their children, as well as to promote familial unity and love. This aspect of the spirit and power of Elijah is so important because earthly fathers affect how people view their heavenly Father.

The Lord said, "I will never leave you nor forsake you" (Heb. 13:5), but it can be hard to believe that if your earthly father abandoned you.

The Lord said, "I have loved you with an everlasting love" (Jer. 31:3), but it can be hard to believe that if love from your earthly father was conditional.

The Word says that God "heals the brokenhearted" (Ps. 147:3), but that can be hard to believe if your father broke your heart.

Many people are walking around with father wounds, but the Lord wants to heal those wounds. He wants to see hearts restored. He wants to see relationships restored. He wants to see families restored.

Malachi's prophetic message added a significant key to the ministry of Elijah-type prophets—the turning of the fathers' hearts to the children and the hearts of the children to their fathers. This profound message highlights the importance of familial relationships, particularly the bond between fathers and their children.

In Malachi 4:6, we find this powerful declaration: "He will turn the hearts of the fathers to their children, and the hearts of the children to their fathers, lest I come and strike the earth with a curse." This verse encapsulates the heart of God's desire for reconciliation and unity within families. The role of the prophet, similar to that of Elijah, is to facilitate this turning of hearts, ushering in healing and restoration in fractured relationships.

The turning of fathers' hearts to their children signifies a shift toward love, care, and active involvement in their lives. It calls for fathers to take up their God-given responsibilities, providing for, nurturing, and guiding their children with a heart of compassion and grace. The absence of this connection can lead to brokenness and emptiness in the lives of children.

Simultaneously, the turning of children's hearts to their fathers involves an honoring and cherishing of the paternal figure. It reflects a response of trust and respect towards fathers, recognizing their vital role in shaping and guiding their lives. This mutual affection and understanding strengthen the family unit and create a foundation of love and support.

The importance of this key message lies in the transformative power it carries for families and society as a whole. When fathers embrace their role with love and responsibility, and when children honor and respond to that love, families thrive and communities flourish. The turning of hearts brings about a ripple effect of positive change, fostering a sense of belonging, stability, and emotional well-being.

Elijah-type prophets carry the mantle of calling families back to God's intended design. Their ministry involves more than just prophetic words; it encompasses the very essence of God's heart for reconciliation and restoration. Through their influence and guidance, Elijah prophets inspire fathers and children to bridge the gaps that may have arisen, creating a pathway for God's blessings and favor to flow.

As we heed Malachi's key message and embrace the turning of hearts within families, we open the door to God's grace and divine intervention. The transformation that occurs within the family unit extends to society, bringing about a collective shift towards unity, love, and harmony. Let us, then, be receptive to the prophetic call and actively participate in turning our hearts toward one another, for in doing so we walk in the footsteps of Elijah and pave the way for God's blessings to be poured out upon the earth.

GOD'S HEART FOR CHILDREN

In the grand tapestry of God's divine justice, a significant focal point emerges—the well-being of children in the end times. As the world approaches the culmination of history, God's purpose for justice and restoration finds profound expression in the care, protection, and uplifting of the vulnerable and innocent souls—the children.

At the heart of God's justice lies a deep compassion for the fatherless, the marginalized, and the oppressed. The end-time justice purposes are not limited to a mere balancing of scales or retribution; rather, they are a call to bring healing and wholeness to those most in need of divine intervention.

In the context of the well-being of children, God's justice seeks to address various dimensions:

- Protection from harm—In a world fraught with dangers and uncertainties, God's justice stands as a shield for children. It calls for the eradication of violence, exploitation, and abuse that threaten their safety and security. God's heart breaks for the innocent ones who suffer at the hands of injustice, and His justice seeks to create a haven of safety for them.

- Provision for necessities—The end-time purposes of God encompass the provision of basic needs (food, shelter, clothing, and education) for all children. God's heart desires that no child should endure hunger or deprivation, and His justice demands equitable distribution of resources to ensure that all children have the opportunity to thrive.

- Nurturing and guidance—God's justice is not only concerned with the physical well-being of children but also their emotional, mental, and spiritual growth. It calls for nurturing environments and loving caregivers who can guide children on the path of righteousness and instill in them a sense of purpose and belonging.

- Equitable opportunities—In God's vision of justice, there are no barriers or biases based on gender, race, or social status. All children are seen as precious and equal in His sight, and His justice seeks to level the playing field, providing equitable opportunities for each child to flourish.

- Restoration and healing—For children who have experienced trauma and hardship, God's justice offers restoration and healing. It seeks to mend the brokenness and bring comfort to wounded hearts, restoring hope and joy in their lives.

As the end times draw near, God's justice purposes are set in motion, and the well-being of children takes center stage. In this divine tapestry, we are called to be agents of justice, extending our hands in love and compassion to the children around us. By embodying God's justice in action, we become instruments of transformation, building a world where the well-being of children is upheld and cherished.

In the end-time justice narrative, let us remember the words of Jesus: "Let the little children come to me, and do not hinder them, for the kingdom of heaven belongs to such as these"

(Matt. 19:14, NIV). As we champion the well-being of children, we align ourselves with God's heart, ushering in a future where justice and love reign supreme and the children are treasured as the precious gifts they are.

TURNING THE HEARTS OF CHILDREN

In the fulfillment of turning the hearts of children to fathers, Elijah-type prophets can play a significant role in addressing the root cause of great lawlessness in society, which is often related to fatherlessness. As they carry the spirit and power of Elijah, these prophets will proclaim a message of restoration and reconciliation, focusing on the vital role of fathers in society.

Elijah prophets will boldly confront the consequences of fatherlessness and its impact on the younger generation. Through their prophetic declarations, they will expose the brokenness caused by the absence of strong father figures and the resulting void in the lives of children. They will shed light on how this absence can lead to feelings of abandonment, a lack of guidance, and a search for identity and belonging outside the home.

These prophets will call for a restoration of fatherhood, urging fathers to rise up and take their rightful place in the lives of their children. They will emphasize the importance of fathers being present, involved, and engaged in the lives of their families. Through prophetic insights, they will reveal the transformative power of a loving and supportive father figure, one who nurtures and guides children with godly wisdom and compassion.

In their ministry, Elijah-type prophets will also address those in authority in society—governmental leaders, marketplace influencers, and other key figures. They will challenge these leaders to recognize the critical role they play in shaping the moral fabric of society. By embracing righteousness, justice, and compassion in their leadership, these authority figures can create a positive impact on the younger generation. As for governmental leaders shaping policies, Elijah prophets will challenge them to prioritize the rights and safety of children in their decision making. They will call for laws and policies that safeguard children from exploitation, abuse, and neglect. These prophets will emphasize the need for robust child protection measures, access to quality education, and provisions for basic necessities like healthcare and nutrition.

Similarly, in the realm of marketplace influencers, Elijah-type prophets will call for leaders to lead with ethical business practices that prioritize the welfare of children. They will urge business leaders to refrain from exploiting child labor and to invest in projects that uplift communities and contribute to the greater good. By embracing ethical standards, marketplace influencers will set an example that inspires children to pursue values of fairness, compassion, and responsibility.

As children witness righteousness in action through these leaders, they will be inspired to cultivate values that promote the greater good. They will witness the impact of leaders who prioritize the welfare of children and vulnerable populations, and they will recognize the importance of standing for justice and compassion in their own lives.

As the hearts of children turn toward those in authority who exemplify godly virtues, there will be a shift in societal values. Respect for authority, responsibility, and a desire to contribute positively to society will be fostered. This transformation will directly counteract the root causes of lawlessness, as children find positive role models to emulate and guide them on the path of righteousness.

Ultimately, through their prophetic ministry, Elijah prophets will highlight the importance of strong family units, where fathers lovingly lead and guide their children. They will advocate for a culture that values and prioritizes fatherhood, recognizing the immense impact it has on the stability and well-being of society as a whole.

By turning the hearts of children toward those in authority and addressing the issue of fatherlessness, prophets walking in the spirit and power of Elijah will pave the way for a generation that is grounded in godly principles, respectful of authority, and empowered to be agents of positive change in a world hungry for righteousness and restoration.

THE GOD OF JUSTICE

God's judgment is swiftly approaching to halt those who exploit the fatherless children.

Take heed, all who dare to inflict pain and suffering upon the innocent and vulnerable. The time of reckoning is at hand, and God's justice shall be executed without delay.

To those who callously exploit the fatherless, hear this warning: your wicked schemes and cruel deeds will not escape divine scrutiny. God's eyes are upon you, and He will bring an end to your malevolent activities.

The cries of the fatherless children have reached the heavens, and God's heart is moved with righteous anger. He will arise as a mighty Judge to defend and protect the helpless.

No longer will these innocent souls be victims of darkness and oppression. God's judgment will shine as a brilliant light, exposing the evil deeds of the exploiters and bringing them to a halt.

The time of impunity is over; no one can hide from God's omniscient gaze. He sees the pain and trauma inflicted upon the fatherless, and He will not stand idly by.

For those who have turned a blind eye to this injustice, take heed and repent. God's judgment is not limited to the perpetrators; it extends to all who have allowed this evil to persist.

But fear not, for God is also a God of mercy and redemption. To the fatherless children who have suffered at the hands of exploiters, know that God's heart is with you. He will extend His loving arms to shield and comfort you.

As the wheels of divine justice turn, let the exploiters tremble in the face of God's wrath. His judgment will be swift and sure, and His hand will put an end to their wickedness.

Let this prophetic declaration be a call to action for all who stand for righteousness. Join together in the fight against the exploitation of the fatherless, for God's judgment is coming, and His justice will prevail. Stand in unity and strength, for the day of reckoning is near.

May this message resonate far and wide, serving as a beacon of hope and warning to those who perpetrate evil upon the fatherless. Let it echo through the halls of darkness, declaring that God's judgment is coming to stop the exploitation and bring forth a new era of protection, love, and restoration for the fatherless children.

Chapter 13

The Double-Portion Generation

THE WAY TO advance the kingdom of God in the earth is through reproduction. In the era of the double-portion generation, a profound calling rests upon the Elijahs to seek out their Elishas. Just as the prophet Elijah found Elisha and imparted his anointing to him, today's Elijahs carry the responsibility of passing on an even greater portion of their God-given gifts to the next carriers of the prophetic mantle.

In finding their Elishas, Elijahs will recognize the importance of investing time, love, and wisdom in the next generation of prophets and leaders. They will learn to recognize the potential in those who might seem unremarkable at first glance, trusting that the power of God can manifest mightily through even the most ordinary vessels.

As Elijahs embark on this journey of mentorship, they will see the ripple effects of their impartation reverberate across generations. The seeds they sow into the lives of Elishas will bloom into a bountiful harvest of prophetic voices, impacting nations and carrying the torch of truth and righteousness forward.

The joy of passing on the mantle will become evident as Elijahs witness the growth, fruitfulness, and impact of their spiritual sons and daughters. They will rejoice in the knowledge that their legacy is not only preserved but multiplied, as Elishas rise to embrace their destinies and fulfill the call of God on their lives.

In this age of the double-portion generation, let Elijahs arise with a heart of humility and dedication. Let them actively seek out their Elishas, ready to pour into them all that God has bestowed upon them. As they fulfill this crucial part of their mandate, they will see the prophetic movement soar to new heights, ushering in a revival that transcends time and space.

May the Elijahs of today find joy in passing on the baton of prophetic anointing, knowing that through their obedience, they are shaping a generation of powerful and anointed Elishas who will continue to walk in the footsteps of their spiritual forefathers.

FINDING ELISHA

When Elijah was on Mount Horeb with the Lord, the Lord let him know that his assignment wasn't finished yet. Elijah still had things to do. Elijah had witnessed a great victory for the Lord on Mount Carmel, but that wasn't the end. Among other things, God told Elijah to go find his successor.

The Lord was actually very specific about the identity of Elijah's successor: "And Elisha the son of Shaphat of Abel Meholah you shall anoint as prophet in your place" (1 Kings 19:16). The Lord was also very specific about Elijah's assignment in relation to Elisha. He was to anoint him. *Anoint* means to smear oil on, and oil of course represents the Holy Spirit. But God told Elijah to anoint Elisha "in your place."

The Hebrew word there is *tahat*. It means instead of, beneath, under, and at the foot of.[1] Elijah's assignment wasn't just to pour some oil on Elisha's head and be done with it. He was to take Elisha under his wing, allow him to learn at his feet, and train him by letting Elisha follow in his footsteps.

Finding your successor isn't just about finding the right person, although you definitely need to make sure you do that. It is also about training them, teaching them, imparting wisdom to them, letting them learn from your experiences and mistakes, allowing them access to your life, and pouring into them as much as you can to equip them to fulfill their assignment.

When Elijah went to find Elisha, he found him working in his father's fields. When you are looking for someone to pass your prophetic mantle to, you need to be looking for someone who is already working, someone who has the maturity to already be laboring on behalf of the Lord because they are sold out to Him. You need someone with a work ethic and a sense of responsibility.

For me, when I felt the Lord stir my heart and say He had called me as a mother to the next generation, I began to look around at the body of Christ for people who were already serving and already had the vision to be part of the prophetic team but needed to go to the next level. I let the unction of the Holy Ghost direct me to the right people, and I asked them to join me at my house on Monday nights for classes where I would be praying for and mentoring the next generation of prophets.

You need to find people who are already committed to the house of God, who already have a relationship with the Lord. I found sons and daughters who were already moving in the things of God and serving Him. Remember that Elijahs are prophets of both word and deed. The next generation needs to be the same. Many people talk a good game, but there aren't any actions to go with the talk. When we are looking to pass on the spirit and power of Elijah to the next generation, we need to be looking for people who are showing their faith by their works.

As a spiritual mother anointed with the spirit and power of Elijah, my journey of impartation and mentorship unfolds under divine guidance and wisdom. In this sacred role, I share my personal experiences, maturing into a figure reminiscent of Elijah, leading and guiding in the realm of the prophetic. The joy and fulfillment that arise from fulfilling this divine mandate are profound and resonate deeply within my being.

Becoming a spiritual mother with the spirit and power of Elijah was not an instantaneous transformation, but a gradual and purposeful process orchestrated by the hand of God. Just as Elijah passed on his anointing to Elisha, I understand the profound responsibility of nurturing and empowering the next generation of spiritual leaders.

In this unique calling, I become a vessel of God's love and wisdom, pouring into the lives of my spiritual children the essence of my own journey in the prophetic realm. Witnessing their growth and transformation is a testament to the power of divine impartation and the far-reaching impact it creates within the prophetic domain.

The path of a spiritual mother is not without its challenges, but with God's grace I find the strength to overcome each obstacle. With humility, vulnerability, and a heart devoted to serving others, I embrace this divine privilege, finding unparalleled joy and satisfaction in my role.

The bonds formed between me and my spiritual children transcend the physical realm, woven into the fabric of eternity. Together we form a spiritual family, united by a common purpose to walk in the spirit and power of Elijah, carrying the prophetic mantle with reverence and passion.

My story stands as an inspiration to all who are called to embrace the mantle of spiritual motherhood with the spirit and power of Elijah anointing. It is a reminder that this journey of impartation and mentorship is a sacred privilege and an opportunity to shape destinies for the advancement of God's kingdom.

In this era of the double-portion generation, the call to be a spiritual parent with the spirit and power of Elijah anointing resounds. I stand as a beacon of hope and encouragement, urging others to step into this divine calling, nurturing and empowering the next generation of prophets and leaders.

May the legacy of spiritual parents with the spirit and power of Elijah anointing continue to impact generations as we walk in the footsteps of Elijah, igniting the fire of the prophetic and leaving an enduring mark on the lives of those we mentor and empower for the glory of God.

PROPHETIC IMPARTATION

In looking at the relationship between Elijah and Elisha, it seems that Elijah was not as interested in imparting his gifts to Elisha as Elisha was in receiving them. In fact, if you read the text carefully, you realize that Elijah initially just tossed his mantle onto Elisha and kept on going—Elisha had to run after him:

> So he departed from there, and found Elisha the son of Shaphat, who was plowing with twelve yoke of oxen before him, and he was with the twelfth. Then Elijah passed by him and threw his mantle on him. And he left the oxen and ran after Elijah.
>
> —1 KINGS 19:19–20

Even though he was clearly not all that excited about mentoring Elisha, in truth, Elijah held a crucial responsibility to pass on the mantle and anointing to the next generation. This aspect of the assignment might prove challenging for some

Elijahs as it requires humility and a willingness to mentor and empower others.

Today's Elijahs will gain perspective as they embrace their role in raising up the Elishas of the future. They will come to understand that passing on the prophetic mantle is not just a duty but a privilege—a sacred commission that shapes destinies and carries forward the divine plan.

The Word is clear that mantles and anointings can be imparted or transferred. Elisha received Elijah's mantle, and 2 Kings 2:15 says, "The spirit of Elijah rests on Elisha." God also took of the same spirit that was on Moses and gave it to the seventy elders of Israel: "Then the LORD came down in the cloud, and spoke to him, and took of the Spirit that was upon him, and placed the same upon the seventy elders; and it happened, when the Spirit rested upon them, that they prophesied" (Num. 11:25).

Imparting the prophetic spirit to the next generation is critical because a church cannot be prophetic without prophets. The church needs prophets. They are part of the fivefold ministry, and they reveal the word of the Lord to the church to correct, exhort, confirm, warn, deliver, commend, and many other things. Prophets are instrumental in releasing others into the prophetic realm.

Paul wrote in his letter to the Romans, "For I long to see you, that I may impart to you some spiritual gift, so that you may be established—that is, that I may be encouraged together with you by the mutual faith both of you and me" (1:11–12). Spiritual gifts provide stability, strength, and encouragement to the body of Christ, and when a mature believer imparts a gift to another believer, it is mutually beneficial. The Greek word for *impart* is *metadidōmi*. It means to share a thing with anyone.[2] When you impart a spiritual gift to someone, you don't lose your own. And while impartation isn't limited to prophets, prophets have a great ability to impart into the lives of others. God imparts great blessing to believers through prophets and prophecy.

When you are walking in the spirit and power of Elijah, you may be reluctant to impart your gift to another, just as Elijah was. But remember, impartation is mutually beneficial. When you are imparting your gift to another, when you are training them and letting them minister under you, it matures you. It develops your gift even further. And when you have the opportunity to see the ones you have led and mentored begin to walk in the fullness of their callings, you will experience great joy at having fulfilled that part of your prophetic mandate.

The power and benefits of impartation are awe-inspiring and transformative. Impartation refers to the transmission of spiritual gifts, anointing, and divine blessings from one person to another. It is a sacred exchange where the flow of God's grace and authority bridges the gap between the giver and receiver, resulting in profound spiritual growth and empowerment.

- Activation of spiritual gifts—Impartation ignites and activates spiritual gifts within the recipient. As the anointing is transferred, dormant gifts are awakened, and individuals discover new dimensions of their calling and purpose in God's kingdom. They are equipped to operate in supernatural abilities for the benefit of others. (See 2 Timothy 1:6.)

- Supernatural empowerment—Impartation releases a supernatural empowerment that empowers individuals to go beyond their natural limitations. Through the anointing, they gain supernatural wisdom, strength, and courage to overcome challenges and fulfill their divine assignments. (See Acts 1:8.)

- Accelerated spiritual growth—The impartation of God's grace expedites spiritual growth and maturity. It fast-tracks the process of character development and aligns individuals with God's heart and will. They experience a deepening intimacy with God and a heightened sensitivity to the leading of the Holy Spirit. (See 1 Peter 2:2.)

- Breakthroughs and miracles—Impartation opens the door to breakthroughs and miracles. It releases the power of faith and belief, leading to miraculous manifestations in various areas of life. Chains are broken, healing is received, and impossible situations are turned around by the power of God. (See James 5:14–15.)

- Transference of wisdom—Along with the anointing, impartation brings the transfer of divine wisdom and revelation. As spiritual insights are shared, individuals gain deeper understanding of God's Word and His ways. They receive insights that lead to making wise decisions and walking in alignment with God's purposes. (See Proverbs 9:10.)

- Strengthened identity and confidence—Impartation reinforces the recipient's identity as a beloved child of God. It instills a sense of purpose, worth, and destiny, empowering them to walk boldly and confidently in their calling. (See 1 Peter 2:9.)

- Anointed leadership—Impartation equips leaders with the anointing to lead with wisdom, compassion, and discernment. It enables them to shepherd others effectively, guiding them toward spiritual growth and transformation. (See Isaiah 11:2.)

- Uniting the body of Christ—Impartation fosters unity within the body of Christ. As spiritual gifts are imparted and received, believers from diverse backgrounds come together, functioning as a harmonious and powerful body, each contributing their unique strengths and callings. (See Ephesians 4:4.)

- Passing on the legacy—Impartation perpetuates the legacy of godly men and women, ensuring that their anointing and insights are carried forward by future generations. It secures a spiritual heritage that impacts countless lives for generations to come. (See 2 Timothy 2:2.)

- Deeper encounter with God—Above all, impartation brings individuals into a deeper encounter with the living God. It strengthens their relationship with Him, deepens their love for Him, and fosters a heart that burns with passion for His kingdom. (See James 4:8.)

In essence, the power and benefits of impartation are immeasurable. It is a divine exchange that connects heaven and earth, bringing heaven's resources and divine authority into the lives of individuals. As we seek impartation and impart to others, we experience the supernatural flow of God's grace, transforming us into vessels of His glory and conduits of His love to a world in need.

When I hosted the Monday night classes with my sons and daughters in the Lord, I let them read what I read. I wanted them to be able to learn the same things I had, to benefit from the things that had helped me develop my gift. I listened to their questions and spoke to their identities. I listened to what the Holy Spirit had to say about their characters. I dealt with their character issues and their hearts. I trained them on how to listen to God and how to stir up the prophetic gift. I also trained them on how to see—some tended to be very legalistic, so I taught them to operate with both grace and truth.

When I was invited to speak somewhere, I would take them with me and allow them to prophesy. I would stand over them just as Samuel stood over the prophets and listened to them prophesy. If there needed to be an adjustment, I would make an adjustment to the word, and then we would debrief afterward. I let them touch my life. I was very transparent.

The church needs spiritual fathers and mothers, but you don't just instantly turn into a spiritual father or mother one day. You have to become a father, become a mother. It is a process. It is something that develops in you as you develop others, as you pour into them. You may not be very good at it at first—Elijah certainly wasn't. He tossed his mantle onto Elisha and took off. I don't think that is what the Lord had in mind.

But Elisha had a hunger for an impartation, which is why he ran after Elijah. He was eager for the gift.

But Elisha also knew the importance of honoring the people who have imparted gifts to you and sown into your life in a previous season. He told Elijah, "Please let me kiss my father and my mother, and then I will follow you" (1 Kings 19:20). Elisha hosted a celebration for his parents and the others he was leaving behind. He honored them for their role in his life before he stepped into his next season—following Elijah.

Elisha learned by serving Elijah: "Then he arose and followed Elijah, and became his servant" (1 Kings 19:21). Having the heart to serve is an important characteristic for Elijah prophets because it helps them avoid the prophetic pitfall of pride. Elisha isn't mentioned again until Elijah ascends to heaven, but he was there with Elijah the whole time. He was there when Elijah condemned Ahab for murdering Naboth for his vineyard. He was there when Ahab repented and humbled himself before the Lord, causing the Lord to delay judgment. He was there when the Lord used Elijah to tell Ahaziah that he was going to die. He was there when fire came down from heaven and consumed the men Ahaziah sent after Elijah. Elisha saw it all. He saw how Elijah lived, how he listened to the Lord, how he obeyed, how he spoke with boldness. It was all part of Elijah's impartation.

Because of that impartation, Elijah wasn't the only one who knew when the Lord was getting ready to take him up to heaven. Elisha knew too, as did other prophets across Israel. But Elisha was determined to stay with Elijah until the very end. He was determined to glean all he could from being at the feet of Elijah. Even though Elijah kept telling Elisha to stay put as he went from town to town, Elisha kept saying, "As the LORD lives, and as your soul lives, I will not leave you!" (2 Kings 2:2, 4, 6).

Elisha's determination meant he was still with Elijah when he struck the waters of the Jordan with his mantle so they could cross on dry ground. Then Elijah said, "Ask! What may I do for you, before I am taken away from you?" (2 Kings 2:9). Elisha asked for a double portion of Elijah's spirit, and it was granted to him.

A double portion is a hard thing, just as Elijah said, because it is twice the work. But it is also twice the miracles, twice the messages, twice the joy, and twice everything else that comes with the spirit and power of Elijah.

Elijah was taken up into heaven by a whirlwind, and Elisha saw it all, including the chariots and horses of fire. But as Elijah was taken up into heaven, his mantle fell. Elisha tore his own garments in two before he took up Elijah's mantle. He was leaving the old familiar season behind and walking into a new season.

The mantle was a symbol of the spirit and power of Elijah being imparted to Elisha. And when Elisha took up the mantle and struck the Jordan River with it, the waters of the river parted so he could cross back over on dry ground. His first miracle was the same as Elijah's last. But don't miss that Elisha had to use the mantle. He wouldn't have known if Elijah's spirit and power had truly been imparted to him unless he stepped out in faith and used it.

The relationship between Elijah and Elisha reveals the power of prophetic impartation. So go find your successor so the next generation can be the double-portion generation.

THE END

In this generation, a company of modern-day Elijah-type prophets is rising, just as foretold in the Scriptures. These anointed men and women carry the spirit and power of Elijah, called to be bold and uncompromising in their stand for truth and righteousness.

Like the ancient prophet Elijah, they are not afraid to confront the prevailing culture of sin and idolatry, calling people to turn their hearts back to God. They carry a fiery passion for the Lord, and their words are like a burning torch that pierces through darkness, exposing the lies and deceptions of the enemy.

With hearts ablaze for revival, they cry out for repentance and reconciliation, urging the church and the world to return to their first love. They are unafraid to challenge religious traditions and systems that hinder the genuine move of God.

As heralds of hope, these prophets preach revival, reformation, and restoration, declaring the kingdom of God is at hand. Their messages resound with the urgency of the times, awakening slumbering hearts and calling forth a hunger for God's presence.

Miracles, signs, and wonders follow them as they move in the supernatural power of God. Through their ministry, the sick are healed, the oppressed are set free, and the lost come to a saving knowledge of Jesus Christ.

This company of modern-day Elijahs is not motivated by fame or personal gain but by a burning desire to see God's glory revealed on earth. They walk in humility, recognizing that it is the Spirit of the Lord who empowers and guides them in their mission.

In unity and divine alignment, they form a powerful force for God's kingdom, supporting and encouraging one another in prayer and fellowship. Their hearts beat as one, bound together by a shared purpose and a deep love for the Bridegroom.

These modern-day Elijah-type prophets are not limited by age, gender, or status. God is raising up men and women from all walks of life to carry this anointing. They may be found in the pulpit, the marketplace, the mission field, or even the hidden places of intercession.

Their impact is not confined to one nation or region; they are a global army, reaching out to the ends of the earth with the message of hope and salvation. They connect with one another across borders and cultures, standing united in the Spirit.

As this company of modern-day Elijahs arises, the world will witness a revival like never before. Hearts will be turned back to God, families will be restored, and nations will experience the transforming power of the Holy Spirit.

God is calling people today to walk in the spirit and power of Elijah. Jesus is coming back soon, and Elijah prophets are the forerunners of His second coming, just as John the Baptist came in the spirit and power of Elijah as the forerunner of Jesus' first coming.

Elijahs are chosen champions for God, for they love what

God loves and hate what He hates. They are the voices crying in the wilderness, "Prepare the way of the LORD" (Isa. 40:3). Elijah prophets will offend the heart because the goal is to turn hearts back to the Lord. Elijahs speak the truth in love, even when the truth hurts. They are not afraid to challenge the spirit of religion or the spirit of Jezebel because they know what their assignment is and they are moving at the unction of the Holy Spirit. They operate in miracles, signs, and wonders, backed by the authority of heaven.

It is time for the Elijahs of this generation to rise up. It is time for them to raise their voices in a call for repentance and reconciliation. It is time for them to preach revival, reformation, and restoration in this land. It is time for them to boldly proclaim the truth of the Word in every social sphere. It is time for them to move in the miracles, signs, and wonders that will cause the people to declare, "The Lord, He is God!"

Notes

CHAPTER 1

1. Isaac Maddow-Zimet and Kathryn Kost, "Pregnancies, Births and Abortions in the United States, 1973–2017: National and State Trends by Age Appendix Tables," Guttmacher Institute, 2021, https://www.guttmacher.org/sites/default/files/report_downloads/pregnancies-births-abortions-us-1973-2017-appendix-tables.pdf.
2. John Thorington, "Is Porn Addiction a Problem in Your Church?," Restoring Hearts Counseling, December 21, 2020, https://www.restoringheartscounseling.com/2020/12/21/is-porn-addiction-a-problem-in-your-church; Tim Barber, "Are You Aware of These Startling Porn Addiction Statistics?," Counseling Alliance, July 16, 2021, https://www.counselingalliance.com/reality-porn-addiction.
3. Blue Letter Bible, s.v. "ʾēlîyâ," accessed June 25, 2023, https://www.blueletterbible.org/lexicon/h452/kjv/wlc/0-1.
4. "Tishbite Meaning," Abarim Publications, accessed June 19, 2023, https://www.abarim-publications.com/Meaning/Tishbite.html; Abarim Publications' Biblical Hebrew Dictionary, s.v. "שׁוּב," accessed June 19, 2023, https://www.abarim-publications.com/Dictionary/si/si-w-b.html.
5. Blue Letter Bible, s.v. "ḥāyâ," accessed June 25, 2023, https://www.blueletterbible.org/lexicon/h2421/kjv/wlc/0-1.
6. Blue Letter Bible, s.v. "šûḇ," accessed June 25, 2023, https://www.blueletterbible.org/lexicon/h7725/kjv/wlc/0-1.

CHAPTER 2

1. Wikipedia, s.v. "List of School Shootings in the United States (Before 2000)," last edited August 5, 2023, https://en.wikipedia.org/wiki/List_of_school_shootings_in_the_United_States_(before_2000); Wikipedia, s.v. "List of School Shootings in the United States (2000–Present)," last edited July 26, 2023, https://en.wikipedia.org/wiki/List_of_school_shootings_in_the_United_States_(2000%E2%80%93present).

2. Wm. Robert Johnston, "Historical Abortion Statistics, United States," updated July 1, 2023, https://www.johnstonsarchive.net/policy/abortion/ab-unitedstates.html.
3. *Merriam-Webster*, s.v. "tolerance," accessed June 28, 2023, https://www.merriam-webster.com/dictionary/tolerance.
4. Dictionary.com, s.v. "tolerance," accessed June 28, 2023, https://www.dictionary.com/browse/tolerance.

CHAPTER 3

1. Blue Letter Bible, s.v. "*qāvâ*," accessed June 28, 2023, https://www.blueletterbible.org/lexicon/h6960/kjv/wlc/0-1/.
2. Blue Letter Bible, s.v. "*naḥal*," accessed June 28, 2023, https://www.blueletterbible.org/lexicon/h5158/kjv/wlc/0-1/.
3. Blue Letter Bible, s.v. "*nāḥal*," accessed June 28, 2023, https://www.blueletterbible.org/lexicon/h5157/kjv/wlc/0-1/.
4. Blue Letter Bible, s.v. "*kərîṯ*," accessed June 28, 2023, https://www.blueletterbible.org/lexicon/h3747/kjv/wlc/0-1/.
5. Blue Letter Bible, s.v. "*mān*," accessed June 28, 2023, https://www.blueletterbible.org/lexicon/h4478/kjv/wlc/0-1/.
6. Blue Letter Bible, s.v. "*koinos*," accessed June 28, 2023, https://www.blueletterbible.org/lexicon/g2839/kjv/tr/0-1/.
7. Blue Letter Bible, s.v. "*akathartos*," accessed June 28, 2023, https://www.blueletterbible.org/lexicon/g169/kjv/tr/0-1/.
8. Blue Letter Bible, s.v. "*krataioō*," accessed June 28, 2023, https://www.blueletterbible.org/lexicon/g2901/kjv/tr/0-1/.

CHAPTER 4

1. Merriam-Webster, s.v. "unction," accessed June 28, 2023, https://www.merriam-webster.com/dictionary/unction.
2. Blue Letter Bible, s.v. "*chrisma*," accessed June 28, 2023, https://www.blueletterbible.org/lexicon/g5545/kjv/tr/0-1/.
3. Blue Letter Bible, s.v. "*chriō*," accessed June 28, 2023, https://www.blueletterbible.org/lexicon/g5548/kjv/tr/0-1/.
4. Blue Letter Bible, s.v. "*māšḥâ*," accessed June 28, 2023, https://www.blueletterbible.org/lexicon/h4888/kjv/wlc/0-1/.

5. Blue Letter Bible, s.v. *"māšaḥ,"* accessed June 28, 2023, https://www.blueletterbible.org/lexicon/h4886/kjv/wlc/0-1/.

6. Michelle McClain-Walters, *The Prophetic Advantage* (Lake Mary, FL: Charisma House, 2012), 81.

CHAPTER 5

1. McClain-Walters, *The Prophetic Advantage*, 191–221.

CHAPTER 6

1. Blue Letter Bible, s.v. *"āḳar,"* accessed June 28, 2023, https://www.blueletterbible.org/lexicon/h5916/kjv/wlc/0-1/.

2. Blue Letter Bible, s.v. *"hāras,"* accessed June 28, 2023, https://www.blueletterbible.org/lexicon/h2040/kjv/wlc/0-1/.

3. Blue Letter Bible, s.v. *"ānâ,"* accessed June 28, 2023, https://www.blueletterbible.org/lexicon/h6030/kjv/wlc/0-1/.

4. "Benjamin Fearnow, "Number of Witches Rises Dramatically Across US as Millennials Reject Christianity," *Newsweek*, November 18, 2018, https://www.newsweek.com/witchcraft-wiccans-mysticism-astrology-witches-millennials-pagans-religion-1221019.

5. Jasmine Browley, "The Rich Witch: This Hoodoo Spiritualist Built a $24M+ Empire Casting Success Spells," *Essence*, June 28, 2023, https://www.essence.com/news/money-career/hoodoo-spiritualist-lala-inuti-ahari/.

6. Andrea L. Barrocas et al., "Rates of Nonsuicidal Self-Injury in Youth: Age, Sex, and Behavioral Methods in a Community Sample," *Pediatrics* 130, no. 1 (July 2012): 39–45, https://doi.org/10.1542%2Fpeds.2011-2094.

7. E. David Klonsky et al., "Nonsuicidal Self-Injury: What We Know, and What We Need to Know," *Canadian Journal of Psychiatry* 59, no. 11 (November 2014): 565–568, https://doi.org/10.1177%2F070674371405901101.

8. Melissa C. Mercado et al., "Trends in Emergency Department Visits for Nonfatal Self-inflicted Injuries Among Youth Aged 10 to 24 Years in the United States,

2001–2015," *JAMA* 318, no. 19 (2017): 1931–1933, https://doi.org/10.1001/jama.2017.13317.

CHAPTER 7

1. *Merriam-Webster*, s.v. "persist," accessed June 28, 2023, https://www.merriam-webster.com/dictionary/persist.
2. Blue Letter Bible, s.v. *"anaideia,"* accessed June 28, 2023, https://www.blueletterbible.org/lexicon/g335/kjv/tr/0-1/.
3. Blue Letter Bible, s.v. *"entygchanō,"* accessed June 28, 2023, https://www.blueletterbible.org/lexicon/g1793/kjv/tr/0-1/.
4. Blue Letter Bible, s.v. *"energeō,"* accessed June 28, 2023, https://www.blueletterbible.org/lexicon/g1754/kjv/tr/0-1/.
5. Blue Letter Bible, s.v. *"exousia,"* accessed August 11, 2023, https://www.blueletterbible.org/lexicon/g1849/kjv/tr/0-1/

CHAPTER 8

1. *Merriam-Webster*, s.v. "reform," accessed June 28, 2023, https://www.merriam-webster.com/dictionary/reform.
2. Blue Letter Bible, s.v. *"diorthōsis,"* accessed June 28, 2023, https://www.blueletterbible.org/lexicon/g1357/kjv/tr/0-1/.
3. Blue Letter Bible, s.v. *"yāsar,"* accessed June 28, 2023, https://www.blueletterbible.org/lexicon/h3256/kjv/wlc/0-1/.
4. Blue Letter Bible, s.v. *"dynamis,"* accessed June 28, 2023, https://www.blueletterbible.org/lexicon/g1411/kjv/tr/0-1/.
5. Blue Letter Bible, s.v. *"dynamis."*
6. Blue Letter Bible, s.v. *"dynamis."*
7. Blue Letter Bible, s.v. *"dynamis."*
8. Blue Letter Bible, s.v. *"dynamis."*
9. Blue Letter Bible, s.v. *"baʿal,"* accessed June 28, 2023, https://www.blueletterbible.org/lexicon/h1168/kjv/wlc/0-1/.

CHAPTER 9

1. *Merriam-Webster*, s.v. "forerunner," accessed June 28, 2023, https://www.merriam-webster.com/dictionary/forerunner.
2. Blue Letter Bible, s.v. "prodromos," accessed June 28, 2023, https://www.blueletterbible.org/lexicon/g4274/kjv/tr/0-1/.

3. Blue Letter Bible, s.v. "*iōannēs*," accessed June 28, 2023, https://www.blueletterbible.org/lexicon/g2491/kjv/tr/0-1/.
4. Blue Letter Bible, s.v. "*ʿăqōḇ*," accessed June 28, 2023, https://www.blueletterbible.org/lexicon/h6121/kjv/wlc/0-1/.
5. Blue Letter Bible, s.v. "*reḵes*," accessed June 28, 2023, https://www.blueletterbible.org/lexicon/h7406/kjv/wlc/0-1/.
6. Blue Letter Bible, s.v. "*mîšôr*," accessed June 28, 2023, https://www.blueletterbible.org/lexicon/h4334/kjv/wlc/0-1/.
7. Blue Letter Bible, s.v. "*biqʿâ*," accessed June 28, 2023, https://www.blueletterbible.org/lexicon/h1237/kjv/wlc/0-1/.

CHAPTER 10

1. Blue Letter Bible, s.v. "*ʾeṯbaʿal*," accessed June 28, 2023, https://www.blueletterbible.org/lexicon/h856/kjv/wlc/0-1/.
2. Blue Letter Bible, s.v. "*îzeḇel*," accessed June 28, 2023, https://www.blueletterbible.org/lexicon/h348/kjv/wlc/0-1/.
3. Jill C. Manning, "Testimony of Jill C. Manning, M.S., Hearing on Pornography's Impact on Marriage & The Family Subcommittee on the Constitution, Civil Rights and Property Rights Committee on Judiciary United States Senate," November 10, 2005, https://docplayer.net/11886453-Testimony-of-jill-c-manning-m-s.html.
4. Amanda L. Giordano, PhD, LPC, "What to Know About Adolescent Pornography Exposure," *Psychology Today*, February 27, 2022, https://www.psychologytoday.com/us/blog/understanding-addiction/202202/what-know-about-adolescent-pornography-exposure.

CHAPTER 12

1. "CH-1. Living Arrangements of Children Under 18 Years Old: 1960 to Present," US Census Bureau, November 10, 2022, https://www.census.gov/data/tables/time-series/demo/families/children.html.
2. "The Father Absence Crisis in America," National Fatherhood Initiative, accessed June 27, 2023, https://135704.fs1.hubspotusercontent-na1.net/hubfs/135704/2022%20Strengths%20Based%20Infographics/NFIFatherAbsenceInfoGraphic.pdf.

Chapter 13

1. Blue Letter Bible, s.v. "*taḥaṭ*," accessed June 28, 2023, https://www.blueletterbible.org/lexicon/h8478/kjv/wlc/0-1/.
2. Blue Letter Bible, s.v. "metadidōmi," accessed June 28, 2023, https://www.blueletterbible.org/lexicon/g3330/kjv/tr/0-1/.s